HOW
NOT
TO TURN
INTO YOUR
MOTHER

Other Books by Linda Sunshine

"Mom Loves Me Best" and Other Lies You Told Your Sister
101 Uses for Silly Putty
Victoria's On Being a Mother
By Any Other Name: A Celebration of Roses
Victoria's Book of Days
Women Who Date Too Much (And Those Who Should Be So
    Lucky)
The Memoirs of Bambi Goldbloom: Or, Growing Up in New
    Jersey
Plain Jane's Thrill of Very Fattening Foods Cookbook
Plain Jane Works Out
Constant Stranger

Nonfiction (with John W. Wright):
The 100 Best Treatment Centers for Alcohol and Drug Abuse
The Best Hospitals in America

HOW NOT TO TURN INTO YOUR MOTHER

Linda Sunshine

Cartoons by Libby Reid

A DELL TRADE PAPERBACK

A DELL TRADE PAPERBACK

Published by
Dell Publishing
a division of
Bantam Doubleday Dell Publishing Group, Inc.
666 Fifth Avenue
New York, New York 10103

ISBN: 0-440-50348-5

DESIGN: Stanley S. Drate/Folio Graphics Co., Inc.

Printed in the United States of America

Published simultaneously in Canada

May 1991

10 9 8 7 6 5 4 3 2 1

RRH

*This book is dedicated to my mom,
Norma Deutsch Sunshine,
for having a great sense of humor.
I hope.*

Acknowledgments

Special thanks to Leslie Schnur and Libby Reid for laughing in all the right places.

Grateful acknowledgment is made for the following:

From *Hairdo* by Sarah Gilbert. Reprinted by permission of Warner Books/New York, copyright © 1990 by Sarah Gilbert.

From *Self-Help* by Lorrie Moore, copyright © 1985 by Lorrie Moore, reprinted by permission of Alfred A. Knopf Incorporated.

From *It's Always Something* by Gilda Radner. Copyright © 1989 by Gilda Radner. Reprinted with permission of Simon & Schuster, Inc.

From "Johanna's First Day at School" from *Night Lights* by Phyllis Theroux. Copyright © 1987 by Phyllis Theroux. Reprinted by permission of Viking Penguin, a division of Penguin Books USA Inc.

ANATOMY OF A PERFECT DAUGHTER

LIBBY REID

CONTENTS

PART **II**

A DEFENSE MANUAL FOR DAUGHTERS

PART **III**

WHAT NOT TO DO

PART **IV**

ALTERNATIVE SOLUTIONS IF YOU'VE ALREADY TURNED INTO YOUR MOTHER

INTRODUCTION:

WHEREIN I EXPLAIN WHY I WROTE THIS BOOK (AND APOLOGIZE TO MY MOTHER)

Dear Mother: I am all right. Stop worrying about me.

—Papyrus letter of a seventeen-year-old Egyptian girl, circa 2000 B.C., Metropolitan Museum of Art

Yes, you love your mother. Yes, yes, yes. You love her; you respect her, you cherish her; but still, you'd rather kill yourself than be anything like her.

———

It is a fundamental truth that, throughout your adult life, you will work desperately hard *not* to turn out like your mother.

———

Often you will make life decisions based on doing exactly the opposite of Mom.

For example, if Mom was a housewife during your formative years, you probably became a businesswoman. You go to an office every morning and work late whenever necessary. You have never in your adult life attempted to operate an iron, a washing machine, or any appliance smaller than a Volvo. Everything you own is laundered, washed, waxed, or shined (if at all) by somebody else; most of your meals are cooked by teenagers in orange uniforms. You worship at the shrine of Free Delivery, Take Out, and We Accept American Express.

Conversely if Mom had a career while you were growing up, you became Harriet Housewife. Your days are spent car-pooling, shopping, chauffeuring, cleaning, cooking, volunteering, and playing Candyland. Your kids do not own a key to your front door or know how to pour a glass of milk. You believe in oat bran, handmade birthday cards, and stenciled walls.

3

With either choice, living exactly the opposite of Mom fostered the illusion that you'd escaped the inevitable. For a while, perhaps even for years, you were lulled into thinking you were nothing like your mother.

Then one day you heard yourself saying to your children (stepchildren, nieces, students, neighbor's kids, or any really short person), "You never think of anyone but yourself! You know what you are? Selfish! All you ever do is take, take, take! Wait till you've grown up, then you'll be sorry you treated me this way."

The tone of voice ringing in your ears sounded alarmingly familiar. Trying not to panic, you wondered, "Where'd that voice come from? Who said that? Is that you, Ma?"

Suddenly you felt a shortness of breath, heard a ringing in your ears. There was a bitter taste in your mouth and your teeth hurt.

That's when the shock of recognition hit you: You sound just like HER, that woman who turned sarcasm into an art form, your *mother.*

Life, for you, was never quite the same again.

Lying awake at night, in a cold sweat, you recall your childhood self saying, "I'm never going to be like her. Never, never, never."

You toss and turn all night, fighting the urge to anesthetize yourself with Valium, vodka, or Rocky Road.

The next morning you have a fight with your sister over the phone and realize that the most effective insult she can sling at you is, "You know, you're just like Mom!"

Then, getting dressed, you detect telltale signs in the mirror that your body is slowly assuming Mom's shape, particularly in the nether regions of upper arms, inner thighs, and under eyes.

Stunned by this image, your life assumes massive new anxieties.

You begin to worry that soon you'll start every sentence with "You know what's wrong with you?" and end every conversation with "Because I said so, that's why."

Like your worst nightmare, you'll become obsessed with covering all the furniture in plastic, playing canasta, or getting to the beauty parlor once a week.

Even worse, you'll start to admire Nancy Reagan or to think you actually might look better in a bubble haircut.

Psychiatrists call this state Prerecognition of the Inevitability of Turning into Mother and link its source to the Oedipal complex, narcissism, and lots of other stuff named after Greek people.

In fact the urge *not* to turn out like your mom is an all-consuming fixation and has kept psychiatrists busy for the past century.

Wasn't it Freud who first said, "Maaaah, do I have to?"

■■■■■■

I first became fearful that I was actually turning into my mother when I passed a Sam Goody record store in 1976 and felt an overwhelming desire to run in and purchase a Frank Sinatra album. I was twenty-seven years old at the time and working in Manhattan. The Sinatra Compulsion, as I later came to call it, brought back a flood of memories of my suburban childhood.

My mother had always adored Sinatra. In fact his records were the only tunes she ever bought. Every Saturday afternoon she loaded up the record player with a stack of

Sinatra LPs and spoke wistfully of being an adoring bobby-soxer, waiting outside the Roxy to catch a glimpse of her idol.

Consequently a huge chunk of my adolescence was spent trying to convince Mom that Ol' Blue Eyes was, like, just not "with it," and for my mother's own good she'd be just so much cooler if she'd only take the time to, like, *listen* to the Beatles. And, like, forget Frank, wasn't Paul just the most groovy guy alive?

So, when I found myself furtively purchasing "Songs for Swinging Lovers" and stashing it behind "Midnight at the Oasis" whenever Mom came for dinner, I knew I was in trouble. Then the day arrived when I caught myself humming "My Way" on my way to the ladies' room at the office. I realized my co-workers might actually have heard me! Panic-stricken, I immediately called a shrink. Within weeks I quit my job and began researching this book.

———

I started my investigations by studying modern popular literature; the observations of such thinkers as Danielle Steel and Judith Krantz confirmed my initial suppositions. On reviewing the seminal "Mommy Movies" of the 1940s—*Stella Dallas, Mildred Pierce,* and *The Little Foxes,* among others (see chapter on "Mommy Movies" for more detail)—I felt on familiar territory and was encouraged to buy a remote-control VCR and charge it to my publisher.

Finally Jacqueline Susann's deeply moving portrayals of mothering, especially in *Every Night, Josephine!,* helped me conceptualize the ideas I'd been considering.

I was fortunate to discover the pioneering work of Dr. Mildred Einstein Gittlestein, a Ph.D. in the field of women's issues and the mother of two daughters. "My eldest works in computers and my little one is married," Dr. Gittlestein explained when I visited her at the Minds Over Mothers (MOM) Institute in Tushey Falls, Montana.

The following citation is taken from Dr. Gittlestein's 1963 landmark paper, "Bonded for Life," one of the seminal works documenting the fundamental ironies of mother-daughter relationships:

> Little girls frequently fight over who has the best mother. For instance, "My mommy is prettier than yours" is a common theme of childhood disputes.
>
> Such attitudes change radically when girls mature into women. As responsible adults who take themselves (and their analysts) quite seriously, grown women often fight over who has the worst mother. "If you think your mother was neurotic, listen to what my mother told me about sex," they brag to each other.
>
> It's no coincidence, then, that although the expression "Like father, like son" is considered a term of endearment, no one ever says, "Like mother, like daughter," without ducking.

As we shall see, the work of Dr. Gittlestein and other ground-breaking psychologists, sociologists, and psychopaths like her, has had an enormous impact on women's lives today. For example, Dr. Gittlestein was influential in urging the federal government to fund numerous research projects working toward isolating the DNA molecule that causes mothers to constantly nag their daughters to empty the dishwasher.

Perhaps one day we will have a drug to cure our mothers (and ourselves!) of this nasty malady, but until then we have to face the fact that we are all genetically predisposed to turn into our mothers and that sooner or later we, too, will attempt to force *our* daughters only to date men who own real estate.

Do not despair. The good news is that until there's a cure, there's this book.

How Not to Turn into Your Mother promises—and de-livers—real advice for today's real women. It is jam-packed with ideas and information for achieving personal growth, spiritual awakening, and family harmony, plus you'll find lots of tips on makeup, hair, and dieting.

As a special treat, this book includes several tests and quizzes (just like in *Cosmo*). You can keep score and feel real smart if you rack up points in these meaningless mental exercises. Many, many case histories are featured so that you, the reader, can feel superior to the women who share the intimate, and often degrading, details of their pitiful lives.

With guidance from this book you *can* learn to pick out your own clothes, have a birthday party without invit-ing your mother, marry a man who wears an earring, and decide for yourself how to treat your daughter's diaper rash.

Follow my advice and, I promise, you will *not* turn into your mother; you'll turn into mine.

TEST-DRIVE YOUR MOM

I know for a fact that the minute I open my mouth, I'm going to turn into my mother, my grandmother or my aunt Selma.

—Cynthia Heimel
But Enough About You

TOP SECRET FINALLY REVEALED:
MOM CENTRAL
THE REAL REASON YOU NEVER GOT AWAY WITH ANYTHING
TAMMY'S ROOM
RUMPUS ROOM
BACKYARD
Let's play Dirty Bad Dolls. We'll pretend Tiny Tears is Dr. Kildare.
LIBBY REID

CAN MOM READ YOUR MIND?

As a child you never quite understood how your mom was able to know exactly what you were thinking. "You don't feel like you have a fever this morning," she'd say with her hand pressed to your forehead. "Do you have a math test today?"

Sometimes Mom would know what you were thinking before the thought entered your head. "Don't even think about punching your brother," she would warn before you had time to make a fist.

You would shake your head in wonder. "Boy, she's good," you'd mutter to creepy little Kevin.

All children fear that their mothers are mind readers. Children often believe their thoughts are actually visible. It's almost as if they think their foreheads are fax machines.

Mom looks at your face and knows exactly what is going on behind that innocent facade. Well, of course, this is no misconception. Your mother can read your mind when you are standing there trying to conceal your guilt because her Waterford candy dish just shattered into a zillion pieces.

The surprising truth, though, is that Mom can also read your mind when you are fast asleep.

This phenomenon was first documented by J. M. Barrie in his classic children's book, *Peter Pan.* Researchers have long understood that there is more truth than fiction in this delightful tale of a boy who refuses to grow up.*

Originally marketed as a fantasy tale for youngsters, we now know that many portions of *Peter Pan* are scientifically accurate. For example, in the very first chapter of *Peter Pan,* J. M. Barrie reveals the means by which mothers spy on their children's innermost thoughts:

> It is the nightly custom of every good mother after her children are asleep to rummage in their minds and put things straight for the next morning, repacking into their proper places the many articles that have wandered during the day. If you could keep awake (but of course you can't) you would see your own mother doing this, and you would find it very interesting to watch her. It is quite like tidying up drawers. You would see her on her knees, I expect, lingering humorously over some of your contents, wondering where on earth you had picked this thing up, making discoveries sweet and not so sweet, pressing this to her cheek as if it were as nice as a kitten, and hurriedly stowing that out of sight. When you wake in the morning, the naughtiness and evil

---

*More recently, of course, modern-day scholars have taken allegorical license and used the main character in the story to symbolize the so-called Peter Pan Principle. This has come to be known as the psychological phenomenon whereby forty-year-old men refuse to marry any women they've been dating for more than three months.

passions with which you went to bed have been folded up small and placed at the bottom of your mind; and on the top, beautifully aired, are spread out your prettier thoughts, ready for you to put on.

Peter Pan was first published in 1911, and as you can imagine, it created quite a controversy. Mothers everywhere were afraid of being exposed as nosy busybodies. Even worse, they worried that their children would eventually come to the same conclusion as Peter and his tribe of Lost Boys. "They knew in what they called their hearts," Barrie reports, "that one can get on quite well without a mother, and that it is only the mothers who think you can't."

So moms banded together to make sure the book was categorized as childhood fantasy. They succeeded. In the last eighty-five years, *Peter Pan* has been sold as fiction and no child takes the story seriously. Thus moms today are still free to rummage around in the minds of their children. Late at night, you will find moms everywhere pretending to be tucking their children into bed while, on the sly, they are kneading away at the gray matter of their offspring.

And for good reason. You'd be utterly amazed at the weird thoughts moms come across during their nightly maneuvers.

Mrs. Anna Winscape of Larchmont, New Hampshire, was kind enough to provide us with a partial inventory of the thoughts she discovered just last night in the mind of her nine-year-old daughter, Melissa. "My daughter's brain is more cluttered than the backseat of our station wagon," reported Mrs. Winscape.

Here are some of the things Melissa's mom unearthed: a little mermaid, the first day of school, chocolate

pudding, lots and lots of TV commercials, chain saw mur-
derers, big words, long eyelashes, an incorrectly diagramed
sentence, second position, swinging and missing, Twinkies,
dentist drills, a pencil sticking out of her sister's eye, Smurfs,
the perfect French braid, Mommy's bra, creepy crawlies, a
Miss America tiara, dead people, Indiana Jones, religion,
hangings, red Life Savers, car sickness, Christian Slater, kissing, kissing, kissing, more kissing, Auntie Janine smoking a
cigarette, babies crying for their mama, a particularly
steamy episode of *Santa Barbara*, a fluorescent-pink back-
pack, aliens from outer space, comic books, a Special Oscar for Best Actress in the Whole Wide Universe, peanut
butter, several pages from *Goodnight Moon*, Melissa's best
friend from second grade, ice skates, being a Big Girl, Sugar
Pops, prison bars, Barbie, being chased, gold high heels with
T-straps, Tom Cruise, liar-liar-pants-on-fire, a pony, toxic
stuff, lightning and thunder, a glimpse of Daddy in the
shower, Babar, bubble gum, Valentine's Day, the Fine Young
Cannibals, small breasts, McDonald's, Uncle Bennie's nasty
cigar, a hungry little kitten, are-you-a-good-witch-or-a-bad-
witch, gigantic breasts, a telephone, birthday presents, not
getting picked, 7-Up, Johnny Depp, spiders, eye makeup,
Gummi Bears, tetanus shots, car accidents, Alf, garden
snakes in many sizes, Mrs. McNeely's swollen stomach,
happily-ever-after, throwing up, strangers offering candy,
Roger Rabbit, snot, Nikes pumps, losing, River Phoenix, hot
dogs, poisoned water, Teenage Mutant Ninja Turtles, ice
cream and M&M's, wetting your pants, fragments of the
multiplication table, Mommy's lap, a golden retriever, a police woman, *Wheel of Fortune*, the Tooth Fairy, Bert and
Ernie, a blanket named Blankie, fishnet stockings, spitting,
snowball fights, the end of the world, Disneyland, twirling
a baton, Nana's noodle pudding, daisies, Daddy's smelly
feet, babies without heads, Eloise, stuffed animals, Mommy

crying, swallowing a fly, pretend, the yellow brick road, Alvin and the Chipmunks, getting lost, Grandpa's wooden leg, gold stars, a big burp, Christmas, playing fair, water fountains, being a quitter, an avocado pit in a glass of water, telling time, Snow White, Ferris wheels, curse words, gym shorts, Toto, sharing, a night-light, bananas, Mommy's laugh, getting yelled at, getting laughed at, crosswalks, show-and-tell, seashells, the last day of school, Prince Charming, sitting on the hump, blood and gore, red nail polish, monsters under the bed, Pee Wee Herman, flying, naps, kickball, Bambi's dead mother, hitting, toe shoes, and a half-eaten ham sandwich.

Mrs. Winscape immediately tossed out the fishnet stockings, the curse words, Uncle Bennie's cigar and Auntie Janine's cigarette, the headless babies, the dead people, Daddy in the shower, toxic substances, all the kissing, and Johnny Dep, even though she wasn't quite sure who he was.

She packed the candy, sugar products, and junk food into Tupperware containers. "The next thing you know, Melissa will have cockroaches," she muttered.

Mrs. Winscape corrected the diagramed sentences and misspelled words, referring several times to the dictionary. She wanted to destroy all the snakes and spiders, but shared her daughter's fear of touching slimy creatures.

She started to throw away *Santa Barbara,* but then realized it was an episode she'd missed.

Last but not least she tried to delete all the TV commercials, but admitted it was a fruitless gesture. "No matter what I do, it doesn't seem to last," sighed the frustrated mother. "Every time I tidy up Melissa's mind, the first thing that pops out is a Clorox jingle."

An even greater problem arises, of course, if your mother is a poor housekeeper. What a mess she can make of your mind! She throws away all the good stuff. This is precisely why you may have trouble, as an adult, recalling specific facts about your childhood. Your mom thoughtlessly trashed the name of that neighborhood kid with the greasy black hair who drove his motorcycle late at night. She misplaced your memories of all those plotlines from *True Confessions* magazines. She junked your dreams of becoming a country/western singer.

Somewhere buried deep in the crevices of your mind are lots of preadolescent longings and desires with your mother's fingerprints all over them. All gone now.

So it's no wonder that, when she's thirty-five, Melissa Winscape will rent *Bambi* for her own children, having totally forgotten that Bambi's mother gets killed in the forest. Later that same night you'll find Melissa erasing all traces of the tragedy from the minds of her kids.

Yes, Melissa uses her mother's mind-sweeping techniques, but we can't blame her too much.

Every night Mrs. Winscape was careful to rid Melissa's mind of the most awful thought she found up there, which was this: "When I grow up, I will never do to my children what my mother did to me." Without this memory to guide her, Melissa Winscape was doomed to turn into her mother.

A CHECKLIST OF TYPICAL MOM BEHAVIOR

If you want to avoid turning into your mom, the first thing you must do is to carefully study her characteristics and familiarize yourself with all the things that go into making her who she is.

Once you understand Mom's behavior, you can figure out how to modify your own.

The majority of our mothers conform to an easily recognizable pattern of behavior. Because they are creatures of habit, most mothers think, feel, and act in a specific manner.

Read the following list carefully to determine the extent to which these qualities apply to your mother. Make a check next to those examples that most typify your mom. (Note: You have twelve minutes to complete this section. Please use a number-2 pencil.)

☐ **1.** She believes she is totally different from her mother, your grandmother.

☐ **2.** She is convinced her childhood was much more difficult than yours. (After all, you didn't have Grandma for a mother.)

☐ **3.** She may grudgingly admit she might've made some mistakes in raising you, but in fact she believes she's the best mother in the world.

☐ **4.** Proof of her mothering ability is that, unlike other children, her kids are perfect—even though she knows their shortcomings better than anyone else.

☐ **5.** She is very possessive about her kids, but often threatens to give them away.

☐ **6.** She prefers daughters to sons, but does not enjoy the process of female adolescence.

☐ **7.** She thinks any criticism of her constitutes disrespectful behavior.

☐ **8.** She cares more about what's written on the card than how much you spent on the present.

☐ **9.** She has a public facade that differs from her behavior at home, especially when she's making breakfast in the morning or talking on the phone.

☐ **10.** She attempts to "keep up with things," but usually forgets to vote.

☐ **11.** She's proud of her adult daughter, but secretly longs to have her adoring five-year-old little girl back again.

☐ **12.** She believes in a Supreme Deity who probably looks like Phil Donahue.

☐ **13.** She does not believe in astrology, but she always reads her horoscope to you.

☐ **14.** She feels inferior in many ways to other moms, but would die before admitting it.

☐ **15.** She works hard to earn a living, even if she doesn't work.

☐ **16.** She believes she was always much more considerate of her mother than you are of her.

☐ **17.** She hates participating in or watching sports.

☐ **18.** She is slightly braver than your father, although she pretends otherwise.

☐ **19.** She won't admit to being ill, and although she may frequently complain about aches and pains, she will never, ever (willingly) see a doctor.

☐ **20.** She enjoys talking about your problems and does not understand why you do not follow her advice.

☐ **21.** Sooner or later she will want grandchildren.

SCORING:

Less than *10* checkmarks indicates that you were not reading carefully and probably forgot to study last night. You are not measuring up to your potential.

More than *12* checkmarks means that you have a typical mother and can continue reading this book. Congratulations!

More than *21* checkmarks indicates that you cannot add very well.

Bonus: If you actually used a number-2 pencil, you are suffering from overtesting in your childhood and should consult a physician immediately.

TYPICAL MOM BEHAVIOR IN THE CAR: TRUE OR FALSE

The road to motherhood is paved with many obstacles. Several of these barriers are in the car itself because in the driver's seat (or the passenger seat, for that matter) many of Mom's most annoying habits manifest themselves.

How does your mother measure up? The following diagnostic test will compare and contrast your mother's driving ability to that of other typical moms behind the wheel. Read the following Rules of the Road carefully before determining which are true or false.

Be advised that your final score will be influenced by the amount of time you've spent in the car with your mother. In fact your driving aptitude may have been inherited from Mom, so don't be too critical of her. The last thing we need around here is another backseat driver.

1. In general most mothers refuse to occupy the backseat. They feel that the act of giving birth brings with it certain rewards, the most obvious being that they never again have to sit on the bump.
TRUE _____   FALSE _____

2. Moms always leave their things in the car and then expect you to go out and get them.
TRUE _____   FALSE _____

3. Mom never takes her foot too far from the brake pedal. She tends to stop and go a lot, which may cause severe car sickness among her passengers.
TRUE _____   FALSE _____

4. The most appreciated feature on any mom's car is the horn, often used in place of the brake. Mom figures that once she firmly honks her horn, she's absolved of all responsibility for signaling or passing on the right. Mom's horn is also used to warn pedestrians that she does not have time to stop at the crosswalk because she's terribly late for her beauty-parlor appointment. Mom uses the horn to remind other drivers or pedestrians of their various shortcomings. In fact the horn is so useful that most moms would be real happy if their kitchens also came equipped with one.
TRUE _____   FALSE _____

5. Moms don't really believe in the concept of one-way streets. And even if they do, they do not consider backing up as a change in direction. As long as the car is pointing in the right direction, it doesn't matter if it's going forward or backward.
TRUE _____   FALSE _____

6. Moms drive 25 miles an hour on the freeway and wonder why everyone else is in such an all-fire hurry. Or they drive 60 miles an hour in a 30-mile-per-hour zone and complain bitterly about all the slowpokes on the road. Sometimes they do both within the span of twenty minutes.

TRUE _____ FALSE _____

7. Moms truly believe that checking the oil or changing a flat tire is as much a male job as barbecuing, reading a road map, or hanging electrical fixtures.

TRUE _____ FALSE _____

8. Mom has the uncanny ability to watch whatever you are doing in the backseat while simultaneously cruising at 75 miles an hour, fluffing her hair, and singing "Oklahoma!" She never misses any of your moves, especially the more vicious attacks against baby brother Kevin. She will, however, frequently miss Stop signs.

TRUE _____ FALSE _____

9. Mom will never admit to being lost, although she'll concede the point that she took the "scenic" route to your aunt Dotty's.

TRUE _____ FALSE _____

10. Mom complains bitterly about traffic. She considers it extremely rude of other drivers to be out on the road at the same time that she has to drive you to the orthodontist. "Where are all these people going?" Mom wants to know. "Doesn't anyone stay home anymore?"

TRUE _____ FALSE _____

11. If there are no passengers in the car, moms will not hesitate to complain out loud anyway. In fact most moms feel perfectly comfortable talking to themselves when they are alone in a car. Actually, for many mothers, driving alone may be the only time they have any privacy at all.

TRUE _____ · FALSE _____

12. Mom's car keys are always bent out of shape from years of using them to pry open screen doors.

TRUE _____ FALSE _____

13. Mom thinks that the other drivers on the road have the ability to know beforehand when she is about to make a sudden quick turn into the K mart parking lot. If not, the guy just wasn't paying attention and should pay the damages to Mom's rear bumper.

TRUE _____ FALSE _____

14. Moms never wear seat belts even though they may insist that everyone else in the car has to buckle up.

TRUE _____ FALSE _____

15. Moms are incapable of backing out of driveways without taking along half the shrubbery, the mailbox, and your ten-speed bike. They will then blame the damage on you because you are always too lazy to return your things to the garage.

TRUE _____ FALSE _____

16. Mom's car may be equipped with an AM/FM radio, tape deck, and CD player but she will still be playing music most appropriate to dentist offices and elevators.

TRUE _____ FALSE _____

SCORING:

All of these statements are absolutely true except for number 9 (some moms not only admit to being lost, they brag about it) and number 12 (not all moms use their car keys to pry open screen doors because not all moms live in homes with screen doors).

If you scored less than 100 percent, you can take this test again in six months.

LIBBY REID

TAKE THIS TEST: DOES YOUR MOTHER DRIVE YOU CRAZY, OR WHAT?

You've lived with Mom for so long that you may not know whether she is driving you crazy or, maybe, you already are crazy. Is Mom the problem or is it you? To answer this question, Dr. Mildred Gittlestein and her associates at the MOM Institute developed the Psychological Evaluation Test (PET). The results of this test will determine whether or not you have a problem with your mom and, if so, how profound that problem really is.

Answer each of the following questions as honestly as you can but don't trust yourself too much. (Your mother never did.) Ask someone close to you—husband, lover, significant other, therapist, doorman, pool boy—to check and correct your answers.

	YES	NO

1. Do you ever lose consciousness or experience amnesia after twenty minutes with your mother? ☐ ☐

2. Have you ever suffered delirium tremens (psychosis with hallucinations of cutting off all your hair) when a relative said, "You look exactly like your mother"? ☐ ☐

3. Do you feel as though your mother has never understood a single word you've ever said to her? ☐ ☐

4. On days when you are with your mother, do you consume vast quantities of food, alcohol, or prescription drugs? ☐ ☐

5. Do you sometimes get belligerent or irritated when your mother repeats the same bit of gossip for the ninth time? ☐ ☐

6. Do you experience any physical symptoms, such as anxiety or depression, the week before Mom comes to visit? ☐ ☐

7. While driving your mother some-where in the car, do you have the urge to crash into a brick wall more than once every ten miles? ☐ ☐

8. When shopping for Mom's birthday present, have you ever considered buying something you know she would hate? ☐ ☐

9. Do you frequently talk about your mother to your therapist? ☐ ☐

10. Do you frequently talk about your □ □
mother to yourself?

SCORING:

A Yes answer to question 1 or 2 or more than a total of
eight Yes answers indicates a *profound* problem with Mom.

Three to five Yes answers indicates a *serious* problem,
and less than three means either a *moderate* problem or
you lied.

However, let's face it, just the fact that you picked up
this book and bothered to take a test in a humor anthology
means you have *some kind* of problem with Mom.

Dr. Gittlestein adds this note: "Don't worry too much
if you didn't get a good grade, don't test well in general, or
were out sick the day the topic was covered. Just remember to bring a note from your mother when you next visit
your therapist."

SYMPTOMS: ARE YOU TURNING INTO YOUR MOTHER?

The progression from beautiful baby girl to a clone of your mother takes place over the course of a lifetime, even though it seems, to many women, that it happens overnight. For some the realization of this transformation comes as a complete shock comparable, perhaps, to a scene from the movie *Wuthering Heights*. One dark and stormy night, Merle Oberon exclaims to her servant, "Ellen, I *am* Heathcliff." Thunder and lightning underscore this revelation.

Without the special effects, many women look at themselves in the mirror (or hear their voice on an answering machine) and say, "Golly, I *am* my mother."

These women do not realize that this transformation is actually a slow and gradual evolution. In his book *Passages That Won't Get You Frequent-Flyer Miles*, author Gaylord

Teehee charts this voyage. Teehee claims there are actually thirty specific stages through which a woman passes on her journey into becoming her mother. The following chart recounts the voyage:

THE THIRTY STAGES OF TURNING INTO MOM

I. Get a pixie haircut and cry for two days.

II. Get a baby doll who wets and demand a full-time housekeeper from parents.

III. Play dress-up with Mommy's clothes but decide nothing in her entire wardrobe flatters your figure.

IV. Get your first Barbie and experience profound envy of her anatomical attributes.

V. During first sleep-over demand that all your friends pick up after themselves.

VI. Change from bobby socks to panty hose, which rip the first time you put them on.

VII. Shoplift your first lipstick, and when Mom sends you back to Woolworth's, steal a more becoming shade of coral.

VIII. Try out for cheerleading, but when you are not picked, decide that all the girls on the squad are superficial morons.

IX. Read *Gone with the Wind* under the covers with a flashlight, and when your mother warns that you are ruining your eyes, tell her, "Fiddle-dee-dee, I'll think about that tomorrow."

X. French-kiss for the first time and worry about germs.

XI. Listen to your best friend (or sibling) explain the facts of life and get a headache.

XII. See *Grease* twenty-three times and wonder why John Travolta never married.

XIII. Go on your first date, and when he doesn't call back, decide to sue for half of his estate.

XIV. Get your period for the first time and spend a week in bed.

XV. Get your first complete make-over in a department store and purchase $73.45 worh of useless cosmetics.

XVI. Get a college education and wonder if it was worth the effort.

XVII. Get your first job and spend approximately a month's salary on new clothes.

XVIII. Get served a martini without being asked for ID and get drunk.

XIX. Make the following discoveries: You like the taste of Scotch, coffee perks you up, and cigarettes no longer make you choke.

XX. Get married and complain about your obnoxious in-laws.

XXI. Give birth and decide to do everything exactly the opposite of your mother.

XXII. When baby starts teething, ask Mom for advice.

XXIII. Toss out your string bikini and white jeans.

XXIV. After children start grade school, think about getting a real estate license.

XXV. When a delivery boy calls you "ma'am," slam the car door on your hand.

XXVI. Discover your favorite song on an *Oldies but Goodies* album.

XXVII. When your husband accuses you of being just like your mother, go after him with a kitchen knife.

XXVIII. Get divorced (or fired from your job) and decide to register for law school.

XXIX. Get invited to your twentieth high school reunion and immediately go on a diet.

XXX. When your child gets caught shoplifting, send her back to Woolworth's.

OTHER SYMPTOMS: ARE YOU NOSE-BLIND?

Psychologically, there are two classic symptoms that characterize women on the verge of turning into their mothers:

a. You honestly believe your life is better than the life of anyone else you know.

b. You can't quite remember the last time you were really happy.

As Dr. Gittlestein has explained in "Bonded for Life":

Almost all women display a remarkable predilection for uttering both of these statements without noticing the contradiction between them. In our work we refer to this phenomenon as nose blindness, a term that can be traced back, I believe, to the German expression *"noses der dumpkup schlupp mein eyes,"* which translates, roughly, into *"You don't see what's right in front of your nose, you dummy."* Almost every woman fearful of turning into her mother is technically nose-blind.

If you suffer from nose blindness, you may find that life can be very confusing. You feel okay one minute and then, the next, you are screaming at your mother because she wants to rearrange your furniture.

Over and over you will be inexplicably frustrated when your mother treats you exactly the same way as she has always treated you.

If left untreated, nose blindness can cause severe frustration and irritability. The totally nose-blind often turn to a life of grime, refusing ever to clean the oven, just to spite Mom.

Nose blindness is a very misunderstood malady and, in its most extreme manifestation, places women in a high-risk category. According to Dr. Gittlestein, women who deny that they are like their mothers are at a higher risk of actually turning into their mothers than any other group.

In order to fully understand the disease, Dr. Gittlestein advises her patients to read the classic horror story *Dr. Jekyll and Mr. Hyde* by Robert Louis Stevenson. "I know this sounds like radical treatment," says Dr. Gittlestein, "but I've had phenomenal results with this method. You see, at heart, the Jekyll/Hyde story is the perfect analogy explaining how someone's entire personality—grooming habits and all—can be totally transformed overnight. In its simplest form, *Dr. Jekyll and Mr. Hyde* is the story of a man who finds himself turning into the person he least wants to be. At first he doesn't mind because the transformation only lasts a short period of time and is easily reversed. Soon, however, the Hyde character begins demanding more and more of Jekyll's life until, one day, there is no more Jekyll."

RECIPE FOR HOLIDAY POT PIE

1. Combine a Mother and Daughter in one Kitchen.

2. Season with a minor conflict.

Ma, I know how to slice an onion!

3. Add Holiday Stress.

4. Cover with a brittle crust of strained cheerfulness.

5. Leave simmering on a back burner until someone apologizes.

LIBBY REID

Dr. Gittlestein discovered this treatment quite by accident. "One night I was reading the novel—strictly for pleasure—I couldn't sleep—when I came across the passage where Dr. Jekyll wakes up in the morning and stares at his hand. Here, I'll quote the passage: *'that hand which I now saw, clearly enough, in the yellow light of mid-London morning, lying half shut on the bedclothes was lean, corded, knuckly, of a dusky pallor and thickly shaded with a swart growth of hair. It was the hand of Edward Hyde.'*

"Well, I thought this was quite a coincidence because many of my patients report that they first notice they are turning into their mothers because their hands look so much like Mom's. I shrugged off the observation until I read the next paragraph, which really made my hair stand on end, even though it was tightly wound up in rollers.

" 'I must have stared for near half a minute, sunk as I was in the mere stupidity of wonder, before terror woke up in my breast as sudden and startling as the crash of cymbals; and bounding from my bed, I rushed to the mirror. At the sight that met my eyes, my blood was changed into something exquisitely thin and icy. Yes, I had gone to bed Henry Jekyll, I had awakened Edward Hyde. How was this to be explained? I asked myself; and then, with another bound of terror—how was it to be remedied?'

"You know, many women, upon recognizing that they are becoming their mothers, ask the exact same questions."

Dr. Gittlestein's late-night observation led her to explore the novel in greater depth. She was the first in her field to recognize that the novel is actually an allegory of every woman's passage into becoming her mother. "The Dr. Jekyll character symbolically represents a daughter figure, and of course Mr. Hyde is mom," claims Gittlestein. The following chart compares these two symbolic characters:

Dr. Jekyll/"Daughter":	Mr. Hyde/"Mother":
Has many friends	Frightens away everyone
Wears normal clothes and hardly any makeup	Wears weird clothing and awful makeup
Wants to marry and have a normal life	Wants to kill when Jekyll isn't around
At peace when Hyde isn't around	Never at peace
Embarrassed by Hyde	Never embarrassed

Other similarities abound:

Like Jekyll and Hyde, mother and daughter are rarely seen together in the same place at the same time.

Each blames the other for his or her misery.

Inevitably Jekyll is doomed to permanently turn into Hyde, and since daughters share the same destiny, they understand Jekyll's feelings when he says, *I began to spy a danger . . . that I was slowly losing hold of my original and better self, and becoming slowly incorporated with my second and worse. . . . I could have screamed aloud: I sought with tears and prayers to smother down the crowd of hideous images and sounds with which my memory swarmed against me.*

Written in 1886 and published as a "shilling shocker," the novel bears a striking resemblance to the real-life tragedy many women face today. "Stevenson wasn't kidding when he called such a transformation a shocker," writes Dr. Gittlestein. "Ask any woman you know."

Dr. Gittlestein believes that Jekyll and Hyde is a perfect allegory for the 1990s woman. She recently told *The Hollywood Psychoanalytical Gazette:*

> I've always thought that a female version of Robert Louis Stevenson's story would be boffo box office. In fact I'm currently working on a screenplay for that very idea, which is called *Dr. Jekyll and Ms. Hyde.* Can't you just see it? I mean, Spencer Tracy was great in the movie version and Michael Caine did very well in the made-for-TV remake, but it's a real meaty role for a woman. My agent is pitching the idea to Meryl Streep, Diane Keaton, and Cher. Of course, they'd all be great but personally I'm rooting for Cher. Wouldn't she make a great Hyde?

A DEFENSE MANUAL FOR DAUGHTERS

> One time I ran out of the store and took the bus home by myself after my mother asked a salesclerk where the "underpants" counter was. Everyone in the store heard her. I had no choice.
>
> —Phyllis Theroux
> *Night Lights*

POWER TRIPS

Throughout your life your relationship with your mother has been a constant struggle for power and position. This battle was aggravated by the fact that you and Mom were always at cross-purposes with each other. For example:

- Mom wanted you to make the salad for dinner, but you wanted to go outside to play. Then, when she wanted you to go outside and play, you wanted to hang around the kitchen and listen to Mom gossip with Aunt Janine.
- Mom wanted you to play with your little sister, but you wanted to play dolls with your best friend. Then, when you offered to show your sister how electricity came out of those wall sockets, Mom warned you to leave Sis alone.
- When Mom wanted you to be her little baby, you wanted to be treated like a Big Girl. And, then, if she ever started treating you like an adult, you longed to be cared for like a child.

These misunderstandings were a common element of your childhood. According to Dr. Mildred Gittlestein, "Mothers and daughters spend most of their lives jockeying for position. Ironically, neither of them ever wins."

Using data culled from her years of work at the MOM Institute, Dr. Gittlestein has devised the following chart, which shows this struggle between mothers and daughters.

POWER STRUGGLES BETWEEN MOMMY AND YOU

Stage of Development	Percentage of Power	Terms of Endearment	Tools of the Trade
PRENATAL			
Mother	100	"We haven't decided yet."	Heartbeat, pickles, cigarettes
Child	–0–	?	Heartburn, kicking, false labor
INFANCY			
Mother	99	"Boo-Boo"	Food, diapers, blankets, attention
Child	1	"Ma-Ma"	Crying, gas
CHILDHOOD			
Mother	90	"Pumpkin"	TV, toys, green vegetables
Child	10	"Mommy"	Tantrums, hugs and kisses
PREADOLESCENCE			
Mother	75	"Miss Smarty-pants"	Transportation, Barbie wardrobe, dental appointments
Child	25	"Maaaaaaah!"	Report cards, door slamming

Stage of Development	Percentage of Power	Terms of Endearment	Tools of the Trade
ADOLESCENCE			
Mother	50	Your sister's name	American Express, MasterCard, Visa
Child	50	Mother's first name	Hairstyle, boyfriends, rock 'n' roll, dirty looks
YOUNG ADULTHOOD			
Mother	25	"Pumpkin"	College tuition
Child	75	"Moth-ER"	Summer vacations
ADULTHOOD			
Mother	10	"Dear"	Telephone, guilt
Child	90	"Mom"	Marriage partner, where you choose to live, where you spend Thanksgiving, Christmas, etc.
OLD AGE			
Mother	–0–	?	Crying, gas
Child	100	"Mama"	Food, diapers, blankets, attention

As evidenced in the preceding chart, the positions of power change radically as mother and daughter mature. As the proverb goes, The child becomes mother to the woman. Unfortunately you do not discover this until you are the same age as your mother was when she gave birth to you.

Clearly, in the eternal struggle between mothers and daughters, mothers have certain advantages:

Mothers are bigger and stronger than their daughters.

Mothers have the law on their side.

Mothers control the grocery shopping, the weekly allowance, and the keys to the car.

Mothers' vocabularies are larger and include a wider range of curse words than yours (which they are allowed to use and you are *not*).

Mothers have legal jurisdiction over the remote control.

Mothers are not concerned with the democratic process, preferring instead to rule by fascist decree.

Mothers can—and do—bring any discussion to an abrupt halt with the infamous declaration "Because I'm the mother, that's why!"

But even very young daughters are not totally bereft of resources. In the following chapters we will explore in some detail the tactical maneuvers that are available to daughters. These highly effective resources manifest in three developmental stages. Early-childhood tactics revolve around the act of pouting. As children become more verbal, they have access to more sophisticated behavior, including sulking and whining. Adult daughters rely most conspicuously on being in a bad mood.

CHILDHOOD STRATEGIES: HOW TO POUT

The act of pouting is one of a child's best defenses against parental abuse. The pout is the one perfect solution to any situation where you, the innocent child, are forced to do something against your will. As those of us who have gone through childhood will tell you, this is an all-too-frequent occurrence.

In fact there are several childhood situations that cannot be tolerated without the use of a proper pout. These include:

- Having to do your homework or any household chore that could be more efficiently performed by your mother.
- Having to share, especially with a sibling.
- Getting stuck in the backseat.

- Being forced to attend any social gathering that will include more than two adults, especially if they are blood relations.
- Being sent to your room, outside "for some fresh air," or anyplace with a sibling.
- Being forced to eat any food substance that is not a sugar by-product.

The pout comes naturally to most children. However, not every child knows how to execute the Perfect Pout. For those who did not learn the technique from an older sibling, there is a program that can help. It is called Pouting Effectiveness Training to Unnerve Mom, also known as P.E.T.T.U.M.

The eight-week training course offered by this organization provides step-by-step directions for executing a pout to its maximum potential. There are three major stages to the art of pouting: Preparation, Execution, and Staying Mad Forever. Here are the basics of each step:

PREPARATION

Close your eyes and let the process begin in your brain. Mentally prepare by saying to yourself, "I never, ever, ever get my way. It's so unfair! I always have to do everything Mommy's way! She thinks she knows everything!"

Ask yourself a lot of rhetorical questions, such as "What did I do to deserve this? Did I ask to be born? Why does everything happen to me?"

Once you come to the point where you are filled with self-pity and righteous indignation, you are in the proper frame of mind for a good long pout. True, it's hard work, but you can do it if you try really, really hard.

EXECUTION

The art of the pout is all in the lower lip and jaw area of the face. Begin by grinding your teeth together so tightly that you can feel that cavity in your back tooth. (Note: Be sure to remove your retainer before attempting the pout!)

Make your jaw jut out at least two inches past your top teeth. Your lower lip should curl downward, leaving room to completely conceal your upper lip.

Eyes become downcast. While in the depths of a pout, you should absolutely refuse to look directly at anyone.

Shoulders should hunch forward slightly, becoming as tense as possible. If you are more comfortable, you can cross your arms over your chest as long as you hold yourself together very tightly. An alternative stance, just as effective, is to keep your hands buried deeply in your pockets.

It is advisable at this point to begin banging your feet against any metallic surface close at hand. Perfect targets include the refrigerator, a wastepaper basket, a chair leg, or a car fender. In the event that none of these items is at your disposal, it is permissible to use alternate surfaces, such as a wooden bureau (expensive antiques work best), upholstered sofa legs, or your baby brother, Kevin, if Mom is downstairs doing the laundry.

Your main objective at this point in the maneuver is to draw attention to yourself without having to speak.

STAYING MAD FOREVER

While in the depths of a pout, you are never required to instigate conversation. In fact all dialogue should be kept to an absolute minimum. It is not advisable to give your mother any opportunity to beg forgiveness, which in all probability she will not be inclined to do anyway.

Keep in mind that one of your main objectives during this entire procedure is to inflict the so-called Silent Treatment upon the object of your pout. You may, however, be required to respond to your mother's entreaties. If so, always deny that you are pouting. Be careful, because mothers can be very effective at outmaneuvering you. In fact moms can be totally unscrupulous. Do not be fooled if she pretends concern by repeatedly asking, "Is anything wrong?"

To protect your pout, restrict your verbal communication to four-word sentences, variations on the following themes:

"It's okay, I'm fine."

"No, I'm really fine."

"I'm not upset, okay?"

Speak clearly and distinctly but do not alter the position of your jaw. Do not express any emotion other than ingratitude. Never, never smile during the procedure, or you will lose all credibility.

Be forewarned, pouting can generate extreme emotional responses from mothers. Losing all sense of moral obligation, moms have been known to stoop to such tricky interrogation as this: "Who wants ice cream?"

Bribery is totally acceptable so long as you do not surrender your pout. Take the ice cream, yes, but do not eat it in the vicinity of your mother. Retreat to a safe haven, such as your room or the linen closet. As soon as you are done licking the spoon, return to the scene of the crime. Give Mom both your empty dish and your cold shoulder.

Learning to pout is a lot like learning how to ride a bike; it's a skill that will never leave you. This is good because, as an adult, pouting will be a powerful tool. Best friends will respond immediately to your pouting, or they won't remain your best friends for very long. Future lovers and spouses will learn that your little pouts can only be reversed by expensive jewelry or Caribbean vacations. The technique is also a boon to your relationships with doormen, travel agents, and hairdressers.

A few exceptions should be noted. Pouting doesn't work when used on teachers, traffic police, or the checkout girls in the supermarket. It also doesn't work in Bloomingdale's.

But, no matter how old you get, pouting always provokes a reaction from your mother. Of course, you may be well into your fifties before you realize that pouting never results in the maternal reaction you most desire, but by then you'll be too addicted to the procedure to change your ways.

ALTERNATIVE ADOLESCENT TACTICS: SULKING AND WHINING

Pouting may ultimately lead to the maternal command "If you are going to pout, then go to your room!" Mothers of course do not realize that pouting cannot be maintained in private. By its very nature pouting is a public facade and requires an audience, however inattentive. Why bother to exercise all those facial muscles if no one is around to witness and appreciate your misery?

In the privacy of your own room, pouting transforms itself into its sister emotion, sulking.

"SO, I'M SULKING, SO WHAT?"

Sulking is an emotional state that can last from a few hours to forever and a day. One woman, Eleanor Featherwell, from South Bend, Indiana, reports that she has been sulking since the late fall of 1988. "After my mother refused to let me spend spring break with my friends in Fort Lauderdale, I decided that I'd rather be sulking." Sent to her room until she was ready to tell her mother she was sorry for making such a sour face, Eleanor quickly turned her pout into a sulk. She has not been heard from since.

"I don't know what she's doing up there," reports Eleanor's mother, "but she can stay in her room until she's good and ready to apologize. We don't allow disrespectful behavior in this house, no-sirree-bob."

The record books are filled with case histories such as Eleanor Featherwell's.

As we have already seen, pouting is triggered by being forced to do something against your will. Conversely, prolonged sulking is generally the result of being denied something that you want. Thus sulking is usually related to material items, such as designer footwear, electronic gizmos, any vehicle of transportation from ice skates to BMWs, and any prospective family pet from a hamster to a pony.

Often these items were promised to you during one of Mother's weaker moments.

"Yes, someday we'll get a swimming pool in the backyard," Mommy says to you after a particularly unrewarding afternoon under the backyard sprinkler.

When that someday never materializes, you go into a sulk.

"But you promised," you remind Mom seventeen or eighteen hundred times. (See next section on Whining.)

Mom tries to weasel out of her promise with the old saw "I said *someday*." This carries absolutely no weight with any self-respecting child, and such conversations invariably end with the child being sent to her room.

Although sulking may sound like a lonely pastime, for the resourceful sulker it can be fun and rewarding.

In the midst of a sulking fit it is perfectly admissible for you to amuse yourself in any way you see fit, so long as no one sees or hears you. You want to foster the illusion that you are entirely miserable and will never be happy again until Mommy makes good on her promise and delivers the object of your desire. Let her think you are moping around in despair. This is why Walkmans were invented.

While sulking, it is often productive to catch up on all those back issues of *Mademoiselle* that have been gathering dust under your bed. Or polish off those potato chips you've been keeping in the bottom of your knapsack. (Keep in mind that it is always wise to plan ahead by stockpiling Twinkies in your room as a precautionary measure in the event of a surprise or unforeseen sulk.)

If you share a room with your sister (a well-tested reason for going into a sulk in the first place), you may not have the luxury of enjoying a private sulk. Pretend you do anyway by totally ignoring the little creep.

If Mom refuses to allow you to stay in your room (an unlikely but not totally unknown phenomenon), you must find yourself a private refuge for your sulk. Try the basement or backyard. If forced to join the family at the dinner table, assume the pouting position until the meal is over. If you are really serious about fostering guilt upon your mother, ask to be excused from the table—before dessert. (This is where those hidden Twinkies will come in particularly handy.)

WHINING

A third defense mechanism available to daughters is whining. While not generally as effective as pouting or sulking, whining does have its own unique advantages.

THE 4 BASIC DAUGHTERS

LIBBY REID

Whining will annoy not just your mother but all members of both your immediate and extended families. Whining is anathema to everyone, including your doting grandmother and the cleaning lady. Whining will get you sent to your room quicker than pouting, which is good because, once away from Mom, you can immediately begin sulking.

The most efficient whine is performed in a high-pitched voice, the higher the better. Try to imitate the sound of chalk screeching across a blackboard for maximum results. Be very nasal. Think of your voice filtering through your nostrils the way milk does when you laugh too hard while drinking.

Elongate your syllables so that a simple "Do I have to?" extends for a full twenty seconds. Phonetically it should look like this: "OOOOOOOOOOOOhh, do I haaaaaaaaaaaaaaave tooooooooooooo?" A simple word like "Ma" can be extended to fourteen solid syllables. Sure-fire whines include:

"But you said."

"You could if you wanted to."

"Why not?"

You'll know you're on the right track when Mom orders you to stop whining. This is your cue to repeat yourself at least six more times.

Unrelenting whining can drive your mom to distraction faster than a note from your teacher and a broken pair of eyeglasses combined.

ADULT BEHAVIOR FOR A NEW AGE: BAD MOODS

Children who spent the bulk of their adolescence pouting, sulking, and whining are likely to grow up into adults who are perpetually in a Bad Mood. The streets of New York are filled with such people. They are known, in psychological terms, as the Chronically Cranky (or Crankpots, for short).

Though they learned the art of being in a Bad Mood from their mothers, Crankpots spend their adult years expanding their Bad Mood horizons. No longer satisfied with merely being mad at Mom, they can now take on the world. Yes, a phone call from Mom will certainly trigger a whopping Bad Mood, but so will many other people, places, and events. For example, a Bad Mood can be the result of prolonged exposure to the irritating habits of spouses, lovers, or strangers in the coffee shop; newspaper headlines; street singers; waiting rooms; incessant car alarms; salespeople who can't make change; dog walkers without pooper scoopers; mail that is returned for insufficient postage; or any form of public transportation.

Crankpots torture themselves with unanswerable questions such as:

"What is the meaning of life?"

"Why was Geraldo born?"

"Why does it always rain when I wear my suede pumps?"

"Is there anything good on TV?"

Crankpots can say, "Go away, pea brain" and "I really hate it" in ten languages.

Crankpots are adept at inflicting their Bad Mood on others. Tools at their disposal include continual honking, talking during the main feature, withholding tips, and leaving annoying messages (or hanging up) on your answering machine.

The 1980s were particularly difficult for Crankpots. Every time they turned around, Donald Trump had erected yet another co-op that they could never afford. Trendsetters like Martha Stewart took all the joy out of having a life-style. And week after week crankpots were browbeaten by *People* magazine with stories about folks who enjoyed better lives, prettier houses, cuter children, and friendlier pets.

Yes, it seemed a pretty grim decade until one Crankpot named Rhonda Sperling decided she was grumpier than hell and wasn't going to take it anymore. An inspiration to grudge holders everywhere, Rhonda Sperling is one Crankpot who turned her life around.

Interviewed in her trailer in New Paltz, New York, Rhonda told this reporter how she had broken the gloom of the 1980s.

"Yeah, it was a pretty sour decade for me," Rhonda said as she stirred her coffee with a nail file, "I was hoping for great things in the nineties. Then I got left without a date for New Year's Eve and threatened with a lawsuit when that idiot neighbor jogged into my snowmobile. It was only February and I was broke. So was my VCR.

"Well, I was feeling pretty low, but then I'm rummaging through some back issues of the *National Enquirer* when I come across this story about an ex-lover of Rock Hudson's who sued the estate and won twenty-one million dollars because of mental anguish.

"Hell, I think to myself, you want to talk mental anguish, come talk to me.

"So, I call Legal Aid and I'm referred to a lawyer who was known to be perpetually premenstrual. This lawyer tells me I've got a really good case because of all I've suffered in my life. She says, 'Rhonda, you've had more mental anguish in your life than Rose Kennedy and Elizabeth Taylor combined.' And I know I'm on to something."

Rhonda Sperling wasted no time. So far her team of lawyers have filed twenty-two separate lawsuits in the states of New York, New Jersey, and Connecticut, all on the grounds of mental anguish. A brief catalog includes litigation asking for the following settlements:

- $600,000 from Mrs. MacGregor, Rhonda's fourth-grade teacher, for not allowing Rhonda access to the little girls' room when she really, really needed it—as Rhonda later proved in front of the entire class
- $450,000 from Mrs. Godley, Rhonda's sixth-grade

teacher, for snickering when Rhonda accidentally called her Mommy

- $7 million from David Zeller, who turned down Rhonda's invitation to be her date for the junior prom and at the same time, asked if he could date Rhonda's younger sister Nancy

- $2 million from Roger Risoto, who lived with Rhonda for six months after his divorce and then split for L.A. when Rhonda mentioned getting married

- $3 million from Joel Aaron Fargoet, who broke up with Rhonda on the day before New Year's Eve

- $13 million from Samuel Francis Markey, the love of Rhonda's life, who promised for six years to leave his wife but didn't

- $2 million from Mr. Elliot, the New Paltz hairdresser, who cut Rhonda's bangs way too short

- $75,000 from Kenny Sullivan, who promised to take Rhonda to the Bahamas but took his supposedly-ex girlfriend instead

- $7,500 from Brian Travey, who asked if he could see Rhonda again but then never called

- $150,000 from Morton Downey, Jr., for subjecting Rhonda to his face one night while she was randomly switching channels

- $15,000 from Leona Helmsley to Rhonda—and every other "little" person in America who pays taxes

- $6,000 from all the personnel managers who rejected Rhonda's application for employment

- $750 from the postal employee who mislaid Rhonda's last welfare check

- $2 billion from Rhonda's mother, just on general principle

On the recommendation of her lawyers, Rhonda is also suing several groups of people. On the record books

Rhonda is the first person in America to file a class-action suit for general mental anguish. She is hoping to win the following settlements:

- $2,000 from anyone with a trust fund
- $65,000 from every guy in Fair Lawn High School, Class of 1966, who did not ask Rhonda to the junior prom
- $47 from every woman in the world with no upper-arm jiggle
- $1,000 from every person who owns oceanfront property
- $64 from every driver who ever cut off Rhonda's car on the freeway
- $2,500 from every woman who is younger, prettier, and/or more successful than Rhonda
- 25 cents from every panhandler who ever asked Rhonda for spare change

Rhonda has been advised that although her case(s) look very promising, she may be in litigation well into the year 2000.

"What do you think of that?" Rhonda says with a shrug. "The 1990s may not be such a terrible decade after all."*

Important News Flash: People magazine announced today that next week's cover will feature Rhonda Sperling.

DREAM A LITTLE DREAM OF MOM

Dreams are the blueprints of our minds or, to quote the learned man unjustly accused of being a dreamer,

Dreams are where a man invents himself.
—Calvin Klein commercial, ca. 1987,
network television, every fifteen minutes

Sociologists have interpreted Calvin Klein's underlying theme to have two distinctly different messages: (a) Dreams are the wish-fulfillment fantasies of the superego; and (b) wear Obsession or drop dead, you idiot.

We all dream and, in dreaming, we symbolically reveal our repressed anxieties, meaning all the really weird stuff we're afraid to think about when we're awake. As the renowned psychologist Dr. Carlos Jungus has noted, "For the sake of our sanity, we only allow our grotesque mental delusions to emerge when we are either unconscious or doing the laundry."

In his classic work *Women and Her Cymbals,* Jungus writes extensively about symbols in our dreams and what they mean in terms of our psyche. He notes there are certain motifs that occur while dreaming. For example, falling, flying, wearing strange (or no) clothes in public places, running hard yet going nowhere, and searching frantically for a dress to wear to your cousin Estelle's wedding.

Various archetypes appear in our dreams. Jungus has developed several interesting theories about these archetypal figures, the "players" in our dream dramas. For women who pathologically fear turning into their mothers, Jungus has pointed out that the most common dream figure is that of the shoe salesman who's always out of your size.

"Yes, he has the fabulous red suede T-straps, but only in size 5," notes Jungus. "Sometimes in these dreams the shoe salesman will have the right size, but if so, only in the wrong color. Significantly, women are more frustrated when the shoe fits but nothing in their wardrobe goes with fuchsia than when the shoe doesn't fit at all. The hidden sexual ramifications and their direct link to the Mother/Daughter/Prince Charming triumvirate are obvious. After all, most women are first told the Cinderella story by their mothers, and when, inevitably, neither the prince nor the right shoes materialize later in real life, who's left to blame but Mom?"

According to Jungus, everyone in our dreams, including the sadistic shoe salesman, symbolically represents only one person: Mother.

"Animal, vegetable, mineral, or monster," says Jungus, "they are all Mommy to you."

DREAM INTERPRETATION

Dr. Jungus retired from practice in 1956 to devote himself full-time to writing *Women and Her Cymbals*. He spent the next thirty years working on his opus, which was eventually published in the fall of 1986. In explaining why it took so long to compile this work, Jungus told *The New York Times,* "I'm a slow typist. So what?"

In this work Jungus makes reference to specific dream images, analyzing in great detail more than 12,500 dreams. When asked how he came to write this seminal work, Jungus replied that he decided to devote his professional career to dream interpretation in the late summer of 1943.

"I will never forget the evening when I had this . . . I guess *revelation* is the only word to use," Jungus told his biographer and granddaughter, Jessie Jungus. "It was mid-August and very hot. Actually it wasn't the heat so much as the humidity.

"Anyway, like all my colleagues I was vacationing in the Hamptons for the month, and on that particular night we were all invited to a rather prestigious social gathering. All the big names in psychoanalysis were going to be there. It was quite an honor for me to be invited, as I was relatively young and certainly not very well known at the time.

"After dessert, a lovely flan served with strawberries, as I recall, one of the distinguished guests, Dr. Margaret Weisenberger, asked me to interpret a particularly disturbing dream she'd had the night before. She related this dream in great detail, and as I began my analysis in front of a group of about fifteen colleagues, I discovered that the chicks were getting really turned on. In the middle of my discussion this gorgeous redhead slipped me her phone number. I thought to myself, 'Boy, this dream stuff works better than putting a lampshade on my head,' which was a little icebreaker I'd tried the previous week.

"That summer I discovered what I wanted to do with my life's work and I dated like crazy."

Obviously it would not be possible to list here all 12,500 of Jungus's dream symbols, because, certainly, Jessie Jungus, the executor of his estate, would sue for copyright infringement. However, under the provisions of the statute in copyright law called "It's Fair Use Because I Said It's Fair Use," we can reprint several portions of *Women and Her Cymbals.* The following selection of capsule reviews has been edited to include those dream images that most relate to mothers and daughters.

Alarm bell: To hear a bell in your sleep means either your life is plagued by anxiety about your mother or it's time to get up.

Aluminum: Connotes contentment with your mother or that you will be eating leftovers for dinner.

Ambush: If you dream your mother is lying in ambush to avenge herself, it means you forgot her birthday again.

Ammonia: Means displeasure from your mother because you shaved your legs in the shower and forgot to clean out the tub for the millionth time.

Anger: To dream that you are angry at your mother is simply redundant.

Annoyance: See Anger.

Anxiety: See Annoyance.

Backgammon: If you dream of playing backgammon with your mother, it means you need a more active social life.

Blushing: Means you recently lied to your mother. A blushing flower means your aunt Rose lied to your mother.

Cab: Being in a cab with your mother foretells a dis-agreement over how much to tip the driver.

Car: Dreaming of a car means that your mother expects a visit from you.

Carrots: Are good for your eyes, even in a dream.

Cheese: Dreaming of cheese, or any dairy product, denotes low self-esteem and high cholesterol.

Clothes: If you dream that you are rejecting out-of-date clothing, it means this month's *Cosmo* is late in arriving. If you see yourself dressed in stripes, it means your hips are expanding. Seeing yourself dressed in Giorgio Armani means you have excellent taste. If you are dressed in a long, gauzy black skirt but are naked from the waist up, it means sorrow and disappointment because the dry cleaners have lost your favorite silk blouse.

Cold: Having a cold or being cold in a dream means that you did not listen to your mother and were not bundled up.

Cooking: If you dream of cooking, try to make it Take Out so that you won't also dream about a sink full of dishes.

Corns: If a young woman dreams about having corns on her feet, it means she will be treated coldly by her mom and that her shoes are too tight.

Dates: To dream of dates is extremely optimistic.

Dentists: Dating a dentist is what your mother dreams for you.

Dinner: With Mom—means that you will overeat.

Driving: With your mother—foretells that you are about to spend a fortune at the mall.

Ducks: To see them sitting in a row means you are given to silly clichés.

Dust: If you free yourself from dust by using Pledge, you will never suffer from waxy buildup.

Dying: Foretells that you are threatened with evil, especially if your colorist has turned your highlights brassy.

Earrings: More than three earrings in one earlobe foretells of an infection.

Elbows: If they are on the table, your mother is about to pitch a fit.

Fight: See Anger, Anxiety, or Annoyance.

Friends: To dream you see a friend talking to your mother means you will soon face a traumatic embarrassment.

Fruit: Eating fruit in a dream is usually unfavorable, especially if the fruit has not been thoroughly washed.

Handcuffs: Denotes an inclination toward kinky sex and should never be discussed with your mother.

Iron: To dream of ironing denotes a longing for domestic help.

Itch: To dream of having an itch means unpleasant avocations and unclean underwear.

Jockey: To dream of a jockey indicates that a woman will soon win a husband, but he will be very short.

Label: If the label is torn, it means you will soon be shopping at a discount store. A designer label is always a good omen.

Panty hose: If you dream of getting a run in your panty hose, it means that you will be wearing slacks to the office tomorrow.

Stealing: From your mother's purse—foretells good fortune, so long as you are not caught.

THE RECURRING DREAM

The recurring dream is a particularly noteworthy phenomenon for women who are struggling *not* to turn into their mothers. Dr. Jungus notes there are cases in which such women have dreamed the same dream from childhood into the later years of adult life. He notes, as an example, the following recurring dream of Jackie X., a patient whose psychic climate was diagnosed as cloudy with periods of heavy fog and mist.

The Jackie X. Dream made Jungus so well-known and sought-after as a therapist that he was soon able to purchase a permanent parking space in a garage on West Seventy-third Street. Jackie described her dream like this:

> I'm in a McDonald's, but not one of the drive-ins, a McDonald's Townhouse. I'm eating a Big Mac and fries. Suddenly I realize I have no ketchup, so I go up to the counter and ask the clerk for one of those ketchup packets. They're out of ketchup, so I ask for mustard, but they're out of mustard too. That's when I realize I really want a Whopper anyway, so I leave McDonald's and cross the street to Burger King. I order a Whopper and fries. I ask the clerk for ketchup and he says they're out. Then he says he's also out of mustard. So I leave Burger King and get on a bus to go home and cook my own dinner, but before I get to the bus stop on my street, I always wake up.

From this detailed reconstruction of Jackie's dream, the lay person learns what psychiatrists have known for years: Reading a patient's dream is pretty boring work, especially when there's no explicit sex involved.

It should be noted, however, that Dr. Jungus used this dream to analyze Jackie's relationship with her mother, who, it was later revealed, was virtually dysfunctional in the kitchen. Called Mrs. X in Jungus's paper, Jackie's mother "literally . . . couldn't boil a pot of water," Jungus wrote. "So it was no wonder that her daughter grew up suffering from a classic Condiment Complex."

To protect his patient from any further psychological trauma, Jungus recommended that Jackie never again go to bed hungry, and if she did, the doctor didn't want to hear about it in the morning.

A diary entry of Dr. Jungus's, dated May 23, 1953 (and later published in the esteemed psychiatric journal *The Incredible Oedipal*), records the doctor's personal reaction to the Jackie X. Dream: "Imagine spending sixty-five dollars an hour in therapy talking about ketchup and mustard. That girl should have her head examined."

Dr. Jungus helped many such women during the course of his long career before he died peacefully in his sleep, in 1989, at the age of eighty-four. Two months before his death, he summed up his life in this fax he sent to his granddaughter: "I can only hope you receive this message, little Jess," he wrote. "I can never get this stupid machine to work. I was never any good with gadgets."

Yet despite the mechanical difficulties he suffered throughout his life, Dr. Jungus compiled an enormous body of work on women and their dreams. Many of his compelling concepts were later set to music and popularized in the song "I Dream of Mommy with the Light Brown Hair." Unfortunately Jungus never lived to hear the tune.

Moms in Literature

Great literature is supposed to be good for you. Every mother believes this and tries to instill the idea in her children. This is why your mother always said to you, "Why are you sitting in front of that television? You're going to rot your brain. Why don't you do something constructive—go clean your room or read a book!"

Choosing the lesser of two evils, you pick up something to read. Did this please your mother? Of course not. "When I told you to read something, I was not referring to comic books," Mom complains. "Why can't you read something that will improve your mind?"

Mothers are never content unless you are struggling through some eight-hundred-page novel that was written at least one hundred years ago.

As we now know, however, great literature is perhaps one of the single most destructive factors in any mother-daughter relationship.

As little girls grow up, they are greatly influenced by the books they read. They come to know the characters in their favorite novels and relate to them as if they were real people. For this reason it is interesting to note that, throughout literature, poetry, and even works of nonfiction, there are very few really good mothers.

As Robertson Davies observed in *A Mixture of Frailties,* "Girls in novels never seemed to have parents except when they were of some use in the plot, and then they were either picturesque or funny."

In nineteenth-century novels mothers were either killed off in the first chapter or described as somewhat loony. It was a literary device to leave a young girl without benefit of motherly advice, often trapped between being a guardian for a father while, at the same time, a candidate for marriage. Most of Jane Austen's characters faced this dilemma. Her leading female characters were either motherless or stuck with a mom who had both oars out of the water.

Charles Dickens, another good example, wrote almost exclusively about orphans: David Copperfield and Oliver Twist, for example. While his Little Dorrit had a father (a madman), she had no mother. Dickens's characters were always longing for their dead mothers, but somehow they seemed to survive and prosper without them.

The Brontë sisters—Emily and Charlotte—created some of the most beloved orphans of all times: Jane Eyre and Catherine Earnshaw.

And when the heroines of our classic literature became mothers themselves, they were, more often than not, severely lacking in maternal instinct. As mothers, for example, neither Madame Bovary nor Anna Karenina would exactly qualify as president-of-the-PTA material.

THE 4 BASIC MOMS

LIBBY REID

Poets were not exempt from these general literary guidelines. When she first began writing poetry, Emily Dickinson, perhaps the leading woman poet of the entire century, wrote one line exclaiming: "I never had a mother." Throughout nearly fifteen hundred poems, Emily never again mentioned her mother, or any mother, for that matter. To biographers she insisted her mother never existed. Yet the truth is that Emily Dickinson lived almost her entire life (until the age of fifty-one anyway) with her mother.

From such writers and poets little girls get a very clear message: Life is a lot more interesting when Mother isn't around. Even popular twentieth-century children's literature isn't immune to this idea. Take, for instance, every little girl's first real heroine, Nancy Drew.

True, she is a fictional character, but, oh, she was real to all of us. How we envied Nancy and her career as a spunky young sleuth! Nancy had everything: a fabulous wardrobe of green chiffon dresses and gold heels; the world's greatest dad, Carson Drew; two great best friends, Bess and George; a hot boyfriend, Ned; and a flashy blue roadster. Nancy was constantly tripping over lots of interesting clues like hidden staircases, secret diaries, and unclaimed signet rings. Of course Nancy's mom was dead, which should have made her sad, except she didn't seem to mind, especially with a gem housekeeper like Hannah Gruen, who was always cooking blueberry muffins and never once told Nancy to clean her room, do her homework, get her elbows off the table, or take her hair out of her eyes.

In the realm of nonfiction literature, mothers are not presented in a very flattering light either. If you think autobiographies are any better for a daughter to read, just check out what Jean Kerr has to say on the subject: "I'm never going to write my autobiography and it's all my mother's fault. I didn't hate her, so I have practically no material."

As for biographies, I have only to mention *Mommie Dearest* to make my point.

So, perhaps, mothers should be a little more careful when they try to force their children to read great literature. In all fairness, considering editorial content, perhaps *Supergirl* doesn't seem so bad after all.

MOMMY MOVIES:
A VIEWER'S GUIDE

Everyone loves the movies and movies have greatly influenced our lives. For example, several generations of women started smoking in an effort to wave a sexy cigarette like Bette Davis. In fact movies have such a profound effect on the viewing public that the motion picture industry rates movies to alert parents to instances of violence, nudity, and general smut.

Many movies have explored the relationship between mothers and daughters, and these films should also be rated for the effect they have on women as both daughters and mothers. To this end we provide the following reader's guide to mother and daughter films. We have chosen the most popular mother-daughter movies and classified them into various categories. Take this guide with you the next time you visit your local video store because not all movies are suitable for multigenerational viewing.

THE INADVERTENT MOM

Bachelor Mother (1939). Working-girl Ginger Rogers is really in a pickle when she takes in an abandoned baby. The baby interferes with her work and love life, causing Ginger to reevaluate her life and values. But everything turns out just fine when David Niven falls in love with her and her baby. He's a millionaire, and after they get together, Ginger gets to quit her job and stay home with the baby.

Baby Boom (1987). Working-girl Diane Keaton is really in a pickle when she takes in an abandoned baby. The baby interferes with her career and love life, causing Diane to reevaluate her life and values. But everything turns out just fine when Sam Shepard falls in love with her and her baby. He's a veterinarian, and after they get together, Diane gets to sell her homemade baby applesauce for millions of dollars and stay home with the baby.

THE SELF-SACRIFICING MOM

Mildred Pierce (1945) was Joan Crawford's greatest screen role. Divorcee Crawford works her fingers to the bone to support her heartless, spoiled-rotten daughter Ann Blythe. Even after her daughter tries to seduce Mom's obnoxious lover, Randolph Scott, and then shoots him, Joan doesn't even send Ann to her room. Instead Mom takes the rap for the killing. It's probably one of the great ironies of Christina Crawford's miserable childhood that between takes of *Mildred Pierce* she was being whipped with a wire hanger by the star of this movie about the ultimate self-sacrificing mom.

Terms of Endearment (1983) is just the best movie when you want a really good cry. Shirley MacLaine is the spoiled, self-centered mother of Debra Winger, who has married Jeff Daniels against her mother's wishes. (Well, wouldn't you?) Shirley cheers up considerably once she's gone to bed with Jack Nicholson. (Well, wouldn't you?) When Winger falls seriously ill, MacLaine becomes such a self-sacrificing mother that she lets her black roots grow out. Believe me, you'll cry for hours.

Imitation of Life (1959) features not one but two self-sacrificing moms. (No, the action doesn't take place at a Hadassah meeting.) Actress Lana Turner sacrifices quality time with daughter Sandra Dee to become a famous movie star and buy Sandra lots of really great clothes. Her devoted maid, Juanita Moore, is rejected by her daughter, Susan Kohner, who wants to pass for white. At Juanita's funeral Kohner recognizes the error of her ways and flings herself on Mom's coffin, thus validating the most ancient mom adage: "After I'm gone, you'll be sorry you treated me this way."

I Remember Mama (1948). A poor Norwegian family emigrates to San Francisco and cheerfully copes with poverty. Loving-mom Irene Dunne also finds time to inspire the literary aspirations of her daughter, Barbara Bel Geddes (Miss Ellie). Heartwarming to the point of heartburn.

Stella Dallas (1937). Barbara Stanwyck is a small-town social climber who marries several rungs up the society ladder and then embarrasses both her husband and daughter by being loud, vulgar, and dressing really badly. Soon she's divorced. Her daughter stands by her, despite really catty remarks from her snobby friends. But in the end Stella makes the ultimate sacrifice, by agreeing not to attend her daughter's wedding. Instead she stands in the rain, watching the ceremony from afar until a cop chases her away. Remade in 1990, as *Stella,* with Bette Midler, which I didn't see because it disappeared from the theaters in my neighborhood in about a week and is not yet at my video store. Sue me.

A Tree Grows in Brooklyn (1945) is a coming-of-age story set in Brooklyn. Young Peggy Ann Garner worships her alcoholic dad and resents her down-to-earth mom, played by Dorothy McGuire. This is a classic story of a young ACOA (which means Adult Children of Alcoholics, in case you never watch *Oprah*). Eventually mother and daughter reconcile, but not until they've both taken a lot of grief.

DISTURBED DAUGHTERS, UPSET MOTHERS

The Bad Seed (1956) stars a chilling Patty McCormack as a preadolescent who kills a classmate for his penmanship medal and then commits several other murders, which really upsets her mom. In fact Mom disapproves of her child's behavior so much that she eventually kills her. Ever since the movie was released, mothers everywhere have used it to remind their daughters not to misbehave.

'Night Mother (1986) features Sissy Spacek as the really depressed daughter of Anne Bancroft. Sissy decides to kill herself, but not before giving Mom a manicure and an hour and a half to come up with a reason for her to change her mind. Mom tries to be convincing, but even after a lot of begging, pleading, and crying, Sissy flees to her bedroom and blows her brains out. This is not a good movie to rent for Mother's Day.

DISTURBED MOTHERS, UPSET DAUGHTERS

Mommie Dearest (1981) is the supposedly true-life story of Joan Crawford's relationship with her daughter, Christina. Based on the best-selling book of the same title, this movie forewarns mothers what can happen to their reputation when they prohibit their daughter from using wire hangers. Many people criticized Christina Crawford for airing her family skeletons in public, but others believe she was within her rights by adhering to the age-old adage: "Always be as good to your mother as she was to you."

The Little Foxes (1941). Bette Davis is the scheming southern belle who conspires to build a factory on a former lovely plantation. She's such a juicy villain that she completely ignores her daughter, Teresa Wright, and willingly kills her husband to get what she wants. Teresa is so upset with her mother that she marries one of Bette's former beaux. Although not dramatized in the movie, it's apparent to movie audiences that mom and daughter don't exchange Christmas gifts.

Gypsy (1963), the autobiography of stripper Gypsy Rose Lee, played by Natalie Wood, relates the tale of a pushy mother, Rosalind Russell, who forces her kids into show business. Just to be spiteful, Gypsy takes up stripping and finds her true niche in life. Roz and Nat reconcile at the end, but not until after they both sing their hearts out.

A Patch of Blue (1966) features Shelley Winters as a totally mean prostitute who makes a housekeeper out of her shut-in blind daughter, played by Elizabeth Hartman. She doesn't let Elizabeth go to school and learn Braille or anything. Then, when Sidney Poitier befriends Hartman, Shelley really flies off the handle. This is a really good movie about a totally unredeemed mother. Great to watch after a fight with your mom.

MISTITLED MOMMY MOVIES

The Good Mother (1988) tries to capture the spirit of the self-sacrificing-mother movies of the thirties and forties but falls flat on its face. Divorcee Diane Keaton gets involved with Liam Neeson, and her ex-husband sues for custody of their daughter when he discovers that Keaton is fooling around, perhaps even in front of their daughter. A very controversial movie any way you slice it, proving that movie moms (like real moms) should never be allowed to have sex.

Throw Momma from the Train (1987). Daughters and sons-in-law all over America flocked in droves to this film, thinking they'd discovered the ultimate wish-fulfilling movie fantasy. They were disappointed to discover that the intriguing title was merely a cover-up for yet another fly-by-night male-bonding movie between Billy Crystal and Danny DeVito.

IN A CLASS BY ITSELF

Freaky Friday (1976). The premise: Mom (Barbara Harris) and daughter (Jodie Foster, in braces) both wish they could be each other (yes, it's a fantasy), and one Friday they magically transfer brains. The adult/teen-switcheroo idea would be successful in the late 1980s for films Like Father, Like Son (1987) and Vice Versa (1988), but its female counterpart is a total flop. According to the writers of this film,

Mom makes the astounding discovery that Jodie stashes bus fare in her sneakers and Jodie makes a few revelations herself concerning the perils of housework. Hilarity abounds as Mom is forced to water-ski and play field hockey and daughter must cook a turkey. The movie misses the mark by about two thousand miles, leading audiences to wonder what numbskull executive figured this as a comedy. Surely it was a man. In reality any woman knows that premise would make for a true horror film.

WHAT NOT TO DO

1968. Do not resent her. Think about the situation, for instance, when you take the last trash bag from its box: you must throw out the box by putting it in that very trash bag. What was once contained, now must contain. The container, then, becomes the contained, the enveloped, the held. Find more and more that you like to muse over things like this.

—Lorrie Moore,
How to Talk to Your Mother

WOMANLY WISDOM FROM MOM
WHAT SHE WANTED YOU TO KNOW
Sex is a beautiful expression of love between married people that isn't so bad as long as it doesn't happen too often.
WHAT YOU HEARD
S-E-X is a vile, nasty business that only very bad girls and normal, healthy boys enjoy—and I don't want to hear another word about "Down There" until you're married.
LIBBY REID

THE CARDINAL RULES ABOUT SEX, LIES, AND MORE LIES

If you really don't want to turn out like your mother and, more important, if you don't want your daughter to feel about you the way that you feel about your mother, you'd better follow the Cardinal Rules.

RULE #1
Never Lie About Sex.

Every time a mom lies to her daughter about sex, a big cash register may as well go off in some psychotherapist's office. Avoiding frank discussions about the facts of life means that mom is chalking up huge analysis fees for her daughter's future. Each lie about sex can substantially escalate a daughter's future indebtedness to her therapist, while an inaccurate answer to the *Big Question* ("Mommy, where do babies come from?") can cost a daughter anywhere from five to ten years in therapy, depending on how far mom stretches the truth.

In fact if mom explains the birth process without once mentioning male genitalia, she can almost guarantee that her daughter will spend several years in love with a married man.

Stacy S. is a classic example of such a trauma. Stacy's mom told her that babies grow from little seeds planted in Mommy's stomach. This might've been okay if Mom hadn't gone on to explain that these seeds were "planted" by a big needle that Stacy's family physician, Dr. Schwartz, inserted into Mommy's stomach.

Thus Stacy's mom neatly eliminated Daddy from the entire process of conception as well as instilling in Stacy a lifelong fear of needles, doctors, and seeds, particularly pumpkin and watermelon. Needless to say, Stacy has put in lots of time waiting for her married boyfriend to leave his wife and kids.

It's usually not until later in life that the patient discovers that not everyone's mother explained sex in the same way. For years Laura C., for instance, thought that all moms described sex as a kind of endurance test.

Laura's mother is ten years younger than her father, and she always told Laura that her father was a good husband because he was very patient when they were first married. "He never forced me," her mother would say. "For months he never made me, you know, do anything."

It was clear to Laura, even as a child, that her mother never liked sex very much. Mom was always pushing Dad away, the way you'd push away a rambunctious dog. "Stop that, Max," she would say, acting as though she wanted to smack Dad's nose with a rolled-up newspaper.

When Mom talked to Laura about sex, she said, "Just lie back and think of other things. I think about what I need to buy and write my shopping list in my head while your father is, you know, doing it to me."

So naturally Laura figured that everyone's mother taught their daughters the Shopping List Technique to Sex, and it's been only recently that Laura discovered that's not true. Yet the reason Laura can laugh about it now is because she was so astounded at what her mother told her, Laura did exactly the opposite. Laura really got into sex and, she claims, she has her mother to thank for her active sex life.

Today Laura is very comfortable with the idea that she is a lot like her mother. (Of course Laura did have a great deal of intensive therapy during her twenties.) Sometimes lately she even finds herself pushing away her husband, Dan, when he goes to grab her, and although she occasionally has the urge to roll up a newspaper when Dan starts sniffing her leg, Laura swears she's never thought of a shopping list during sex in her life.

It is a strange phenomenon that sex is one area where moms feel perfectly justified in lying through their teeth, and they don't feel the least bit guilty for it either. If questioned later in life, moms will claim they only lied to protect their children. In fact one of the remarkable advantages about motherhood is always being able to weasel out of your mistakes by saying, "I only did it for your own good, dear."

The noted psychiatrist Dr. Janis Panis described the results of being taught sexual falsehoods in childhood in her 1954 work, *Recollection, Repression, and the Result of Telling Whoppers:* "The good news is eventually we discover that everything our mothers told us about sex was absolutely wrong. The bad news is we make this discovery when we are thirty-seven years old."

RULE #2
Give Good Gifts.

Our mother's first gift to us comes at the moment we are born, because Mom, as she will subsequently remind us over and over, gives us the Gift of Life. Like many of the gifts we receive from our mothers, the Gift of Life usually doesn't fit properly and is almost never returnable without a major hassle.

Later in life Mom will give many gifts that are symbolic of her unconsciously hostile feelings toward us. Dr. Mildred Gittlestein described this phenomenon in a paper entitled "Hostility and the Holidays: Gifts Between Mothers and Daughters" (MOM Press, 1964).

The "Happy Birthday" paper, as it has come to be known, traces the history of Anna B., a single woman and one of the first women treated at the MOM Institute for manic depression, erratic sleep patterns, and excessive facial hair. In this paper Dr. Gittlestein brilliantly demonstrates that Anna B.'s mother was up to no good when, for Anna's fortieth birthday, she mailed her daughter a copy of *1,001 Ways to Play Solitaire*, along with a deck of American Airlines playing cards.

Dr. Gittlestein analyzed this gift in the context of its psycho-sexual-phobic-aerobic meaning: "Anna was an only child, unmarried and this was her Big Four-O, so you'd think her mother would spend more than a lousy three bucks on a gift. Talk about your cheapskates!"

RULE #3
Learn the Specifics.

It's all well and good to claim an interest in your daughter's life, but in order to prove that you really do

care, moms should get the facts straight. Be not only atten-
tive but retentive. Ask questions, if you must, but not the
same ones over and over.

The frustration of having a mother who doesn't listen
was clearly articulated by Eve W., a thirty-two-year-old career woman living in Hoboken, New Jersey, and working
in Manhattan. Eve described her mother's fatal flaw at a
recent gathering of singles in a sleazy Upper East Side bar:

"I like my work. I've had the same job for five years
and my mother always says she's proud of me. I talk about
my work all the time and my mother acts interested in
what I'm saying. She proudly tells everyone, 'My daughter,
Eve, is a big-shot publicist at a big publishing house.'

"Her friends smile and say, 'How nice, but what does
a publicist do exactly?'

" 'I don't know,' my mother always says. 'Eve, tell the
ladies what it is you do, exactly.'

"It drives me crazy that she never remembers what I
do for a living, even though I've explained it to her a hundred times. Here she hands out my business cards like pea-
nuts to everyone she knows, yet she can't actually describe
my job to anyone!"

One of the things that makes daughters really crazy is
the inability of their mothers to retain basic facts and details
about their own children while being able to recite convo-
luted plot lines from *Falcon Crest* and *Days of Our Lives*
without a hitch.

Anyone who wishes *not* to turn into her mother
should remember to really remember what her daughter
tells her.

RULE #4

Grow Up, Already! Quit Blaming Mom for Every Little Thing.

In the very first weeks of life your mother will teach you (through looks, physical contact, and tone of voice) how to be submissive, to suppress your true feelings, and to control your anger, all of which will prepare you in later life to do meaningless, repetitive work in an office, factory, or kitchen.

As an adolescent you will begin to think that everything you don't like about yourself is your mother's fault. You blame mom for everything, and this becomes very habit-forming for you as an adult.

But remember, someday you will want your daughter to forgive you for messing up her life, so before that happens, show the world you can be a sport. Forgive your mother and remember that even if you have a terrible relationship with mom, there is a gift in what she gave you.

See, mom taught you how to be secretive and hide your true self from her disapproving eyes. Thanks to mom, throughout your life you will search for someone who can disapprove of you as strongly as your mother, and when you find that special person, you will probably marry him.

HOW NOT TO LOOK LIKE YOUR MOTHER

In a recent survey conducted by WHOWSO (Women Helping Other Women, Sort Of), over 44,000 women of varying ages, economic brackets, marital status, and estrogen levels were asked the following multiple-choice question:

Whom do you most resemble:
  (a) Roseanne Barr
  (b) Jane Fonda
  (c) Your mother

Remarkably, 95.6 percent of all women answered (b) Jane Fonda; 4 percent answered (a) Roseanne Barr; and the remaining 0.4 percent described themselves as radical feminists protesting the fact we didn't include Harry Hamlin as one of the choices.

Sociologists have speculated that even with the popularity of *Jane Fonda's Workout* videotapes, records, books,
leotards, and divorce proceedings, even if women did Jane
Fonda every day of their lives and watched *On Golden Pond*
three times a week, even then, it's unlikely that more than
two or three of them would ever actually achieve the
Fonda flat stomach—not to mention her inner thighs and
hips. Let's face it, most of us do look more like Roseanne
Barr than Ms. Fonda. Thus we must conclude that most
women are living in complete denial.

What's really interesting, though, about this survey is
that *not one* respondent would admit to looking like the
woman who gave birth to her.

Why do so few women (actually none at all) acknowledge any resemblance to their mothers? The answer is
simple. Women don't want to look like their mothers, because they don't want to be like their mothers.

In her formative years a female becomes aware that
no matter what one wants to achieve in life—from cheer-
leader to MBA to Mrs.—it is always wise to remember that
Looks Count, A LOT! We learn this from our mothers
through what is called the Embarrassment Quotient. This
is defined as the degree to which Mom embarrassed you
because of her ineptitude in the three major Looks Categories, that is, makeup, hair, and clothing. In the competitive
world of grade school, for example, we soon discovered
that whether or not Mom was late in arriving for the school
play was not nearly so important as the brand of designer
jeans she was wearing.

So, obviously, one of the fundamental methods to
avoid turning out like your mother is to make certain that
you do not resemble her in any way. Forget the forties
look, forget antique clothing (unless you want to go back
to Grandma's generation), forget retro.

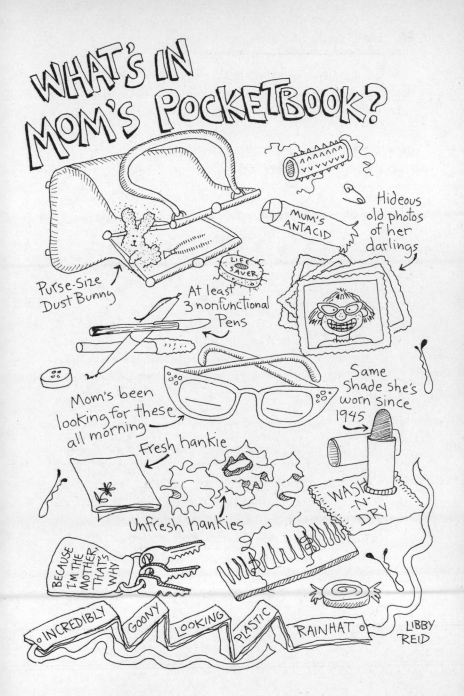

Concentrate on developing your own style, or someday your daughter will say to you, "Ma, you look like a geek
in that dress. Can't Daddy drive us to the mall?"

DO'S AND DON'TS OF DRESSING (BUT MAINLY DON'TS)

1. Don't put a whole pound of rouge on your cheeks and
   say, "Oh, it'll wear off soon enough."
2. Don't tease the top of your hair so much that you
   leave a big hole in the back, as if no one ever sees you
   from behind.
3. Don't use half a bottle of perfume every time you go
   into the bathroom.
4. Don't color-coordinate your shoes, handbag, earrings,
   handkerchief, and hair ribbon.
5. Don't leave the house with your hair in those stupid
   pink rollers. To be safe, don't leave your bathroom.
6. Don't dress in the same clothes as your daughter, especially if she is under the age of thirty-three.
7. Don't use makeup to make little points at the tops of
   your lips or little triangles at the corner of your eyes.
8. Don't pencil eyebrows over your real brows.
9. Don't ever smudge lipstick on your teeth.
10. Don't ever use orange-colored foundation base, es-
    pecially if you apply it only as far down as your jawline
    so that you have real dark cheeks and a white, white
    neck.
11. Don't shave your legs without using water.
12. Don't rub your eyes two seconds after applying eye-
    liner.
13. Never expose undergarments (bra straps, for exam-
    ple) to public scrutiny if you are over voting age.
14. Do not wear any garment made of stretch material,

especially any apparel that exposes upper arms or outlines outer thighs. Only wear exercise clothes (sweatpants, leotards, etc.) if you exercise regularly.

15. Avoid wearing rhinestones, sequins, or metallic colors before sunset.

WHAT NOT *TO SAY* *. . . EVER, EVER, EVER*

Your memory bank is like a massive computer where a ton of information is stored. Also stored up there are your mother's words and expressions, which are like glitches in your data storage. These are expressions you *hated* as a kid, and guaranteed, these are the same expressions your kids will hate hearing from you.

If you want to avoid turning out like your mother, there are several common expressions that you must permanently delete from your vocabulary.

Once you've uttered any of the following lines, you are well on the way to becoming your mother.

1. "What am I signing?"
2. "As long as you're going out, take out the garbage."
3. "Am I going to be picking up wet towels for the rest of my life?"
4. "You could poke out an eye doing that!"

5. "If I ever talked to my mother the way you talk to me, I wouldn't be able to sit down for a week."
6. "If I didn't love you, I wouldn't care."
7. "Everything was so much better in my day; the people were nicer, the streets were cleaner, the food tasted better."
8. "Everything was so much harder in my day; we didn't have half the luxuries you have."
9. "Daddy always wanted a son."
10. "No one will ever love you like your mother!"
11. "I'll give you something to cry about."
12. "This is not what I sent you to college for."
13. "Your mother always knows what's best."
14. "I'm not made of money."
15. "Your sister is the pretty one."
16. "Hair grows back."
17. "Erase doesn't really hide those blemishes."
18. "You can't change the past."
19. "They're both the same so don't fight with your brother."
20. "Don't worry, darling, you have a great personality."
21. "Someday you'll need algebra."
22. "I sacrificed everything for my children."
23. "You're just like me!"
24. "These are the best years of your life."
25. "You call this Christmas music?"
26. "You know what the trouble with you is?"
27. "I'm telling you this for your own good."
28. "Don't you ever, as long as you live, talk to me like that again."
29. "Don't put anything around your neck, even as a joke!"
30. "Nothing wears a piece of furniture out quicker than leaving it in the same place."
31. "I'm still your mother, you know."

32. "The apple doesn't fall far from the tree."
33. "Monsters? That's silly!"
34. "How dare you?"
35. "Who do you think you are?"
36. "Share and share alike."

WHAT NOT
TO CRITICIZE

Your childhood education is a cherished combination of Mom's memorable scoldings, recriminations, and punishments; dialogue from *The Mary Tyler Moore Show* and reruns of *Leave It to Beaver* and *Bewitched*; maxims from Dubble Bubble gum; romance comics; *True Confession* magazines; and the racier passages of novels like *Lady Chatterley's Lover* and *Peyton Place*. Yet of all these varied influences, perhaps the most damaging are Mom's criticisms. Many of us would prefer a week of after-school detention to one of Mom's biting remarks.

Mothers are notorious for being totally honest with their daughters, even when a bit of downright fabrication would go a long way. "That's not a scratch on your face," mothers will insist, "you've been squeezing blackheads again!"

Even when we try really hard to please, moms have a way of undercutting our best efforts. We attempt to make dinner and Mom faults us for roasting the chicken upside down. If we do Mom the favor of putting through the laundry, she gets upset just because the washing machine overloaded and flooded the basement. And she's so critical when we're a few months late in returning a videotape to the rental store.

And Mom's criticisms are not the only burden daughters have to bear. Many times Mom's enthusiasm is just as difficult to take. This is because mothers tend to negate even a so-called compliment with the deadly qualifier "Of course *I* think your Science Fair project looks fine. *I'm* your mother."

HOW GOOD ARE YOU AT DEFLECTING MOM'S CRITICISMS?

Many of us compound the problem of maternal criticism by never learning from our past mistakes. We are victims of a virtually incurable condition called the Etcetera syndrome, which was documented in 1987 by Dr. P. H. Dee, a colleague of Dr. Gittlestein at the MOM Institute.

Dr. Dee was the first in her field to recognize the Etcetera syndrome, which she defined as "the process of continually repeating the same mistake over and over and over again until you just want to puke."

Dr. Dee published a brilliant examination of this theory in her near-classic book, *The Repetition Complex, The Repetition Complex, The Repetition Complex.*

A prime example of this syndrome can be found in the following case study, which took place one afternoon between a patient Dr. Dee called Irma and Irma's mother. Irma and her mother have what many experts call a "good enough" relationship. That is, they see each other at least once a month and Irma returns her mother's phone calls approximately 75 percent of the time. Yet Irma, like many women, is particularly inept at deflecting her mother's criticisms. She tends to make needless errors, which only promote even more maternal criticisms.

Read the following case study carefully and see if you can spot Irma's mistakes. According to Dr. Dee's calculations, within a span of only a few hours Irma made five Major Mom Mistakes, all of which could've been avoided if Irma had taken a few simple precautions.

Can you spot Irma's errors?

ANOTHER TEST

Irma is a very successful executive working on Wall Street. She is happily married (well, relatively happily married) and recently she and her husband purchased a co-op in a brownstone on one of the trendiest streets in Brooklyn Heights. Irma was really proud of her new apartment and wanted to show it to her mother. She invited Mom for Sunday dinner.

At 11:00 A.M. the doorbell rang. Irma's mother arrived four hours early (which she did whenever she was invited anywhere). "Ma, I told you dinner was at three," Irma complained.

"I was worried about traffic," Mom replied, "so I left home a little early. And I can't believe you're still in your bathrobe."

Irma offered to make her mother a cup of tea. In her brand-new, eat-in kitchen, Irma asked, "So, Ma, what do you think of the kitchen?"

Mom scanned the kitchen without saying anything. Then she pointed to a bag of Cornucopia cat food on the counter. "So, now you're a Yuppie, you buy that expensive brand."

Irma decided to ignore the remark and lead her mother into the dining room, where Mom remarked, "Darling, that dining room table has got to go!"

In the living room her mom said, "You know, this place is much smaller than the way you described it."

While eating dinner, Irma wondered why she'd wanted to invite her mother over in the first place.

"You know," Mom said, "this spaghetti sauce, it's missing something. Are you sure you used enough salt?"

■■■■■■

Now, what were Irma's mistakes?

■■■■■■

First, Irma should never have invited her mother for both an apartment inspection and dinner. It is always advisable to limit the opportunities for criticism that we present to our mothers. Irma should've invited her mother for a quick inspection before she actually moved into the apartment so that by the time she was ready to invite her mother for dinner, Mom would've gotten her major negative comments out of her system.

Second, Irma left herself open for a serious critical attack when she asked, "So, Ma, what do you think?"

Mothers feel free enough to tell us what they think without any prompting, thank you very much.

Third, Irma wasted valuable fantasy time wondering why she'd invited Mom in the first place. As mature women we must acknowledge the great paradox of our adult life: No matter how many times we disagree with our mothers; no matter how lacking our mothers are in taste, style, or sophistication; no matter how much we doubt our mother's intelligence, perception, or sensitivity; no matter how much we disapprove of our mothers—nothing is more crucial to us than our mother's approval. Nothing.

In *Memoirs of a Dutiful Daughter* (the title tells you a lot), the brilliant French writer Simone de Beauvoir tells us that "any reproach made by my mother, and even her slightest frown, was a threat to my security: without her approval, I no longer felt I had the right to live." Which only goes to prove that this condition is international in scope.

Eventually, of course, we discover we need Mom's approval like we need another dollop of cellulite, but we don't come to that particular realization until we've spent approximately $45,000 in therapy fees. (See chapter called "Seeking Professional Help: Analysis, Paralysis" for further details.)

Fourth, Irma served her mother a good meal. It is always best to conceal from your mother the fact that you can cook. If not, you severely threaten Mom's fantasy of being the only woman in the world who can make a decent spaghetti sauce. If Irma had served frozen fish sticks, re-heated fries, and canned fruit cocktail, her mom would never have complained about the food.

And finally Irma really goofed when she bought a co-op in Brooklyn Heights, especially since she and her husband had to borrow cash for the down payment, but as Mom would say, that's another kettle of fish altogether.

AN OUNCE OF PREVENTION: ADVICE TO MOTHERS OF DAUGHTERS

Can mothers stop themselves from being so critical of their daughters? Is there ever a point in the relationship when mothers say, "Okay, darling, you can stop trying so hard. You are perfect exactly as you are. I'm completely satisfied with everything about you."

Conversely, can daughters ever outgrow Mom's critical eye?

These questions are crucial to any woman who does not want to turn into her mother.

For daughters the issue isn't whether or not we can endure yet another minor slight or hurt feeling. The problem is that we tend to carry our mothers' criticisms with us for the rest of our lives.

Take the case history of Laurie Lestoil. While shopping for a bathing suit in May, 1974, Laurie's mother remarked, "You know, sweetheart, from the knees down, your legs aren't so bad."

Laurie said nothing. In fact she mentally blocked out the entire day, and it was not until much later in her life, after years of therapy, that Laurie was able to recall the incident. Yet even after intensive therapy, because of her mother's remark, Laurie carried with her some permanent scars that greatly affected her work.

A successful writer, Laurie received an exciting call from her agent one day. "Laurie, darling heart, two Hollywood producers want to take a meeting with us. They're interested in buying the film rights to your novel *Heart Attack at the Oasis.* Isn't that fabulous? Be here at my office next Thursday at four o'clock. And darling, remember the first rule of making film deals: Let your agent do all the talking. See you!"

So, Laurie Lestoil "took" her first meeting. The two Hollywood producers were very enthusiastic, very young women who constantly dropped names like Meg Ryan and Goldie Hawn.

Laurie nodded and smiled.

"Don't you think Richard Lewis would be fabulous for the role of Seymour?" one of them asked.

"Fabulous!" exclaimed Laurie's agent.

Laurie nodded and smiled, nodded and smiled.

The producers promised to show the property to Bette Midler's "people," whoever they were.

"I guess I should be thinking how much this could mean to my career," Laurie mused to herself as the meeting progressed to a heated debate over percentage points and grosses. Instead Laurie was troubled by this observation: "Every woman in this room has thinner thighs than me."

Laurie found herself in the throes of full-blown lower-body anxiety attack.

After the meeting Laurie raced to her therapist's office to tell Dr. Cecilia Yesandno how she, Laurie, had once again sabotaged yet another opportunity to feel happy.

"They wanted to discuss rewrites and sequels," Laurie moaned. "I wanted to ask where they aerobized."

Cecilia explained to Laurie how all of these feelings were related to her relationship with her mother, how Laurie had learned to treat herself this way from a very early age.

"Remember your mother's remark in the dressing room at B. Altman? Well, this incident today just proves that you've never fully worked through that vicious attack on your hips and thighs."

This was a broken record with Cecilia, so Laurie didn't feel compelled to listen too closely. In fact Laurie became even more agitated by another revelation she had that afternoon when she suddenly realized that her thighs were even fatter than Cecilia's.

"Maybe I should try a male shrink," Laurie thought to herself. "A really overweight male shrink."

The moral to this case study is that any criticism by a mother can generate a severe, profound, and everlasting trauma to a daughter's self-image. Even Mom's casual remarks, thrown off without thinking, can haunt a daughter for the rest of her life.

Therefore mothers need to be very careful when offering any and all criticisms. Let's take a few moments to examine some general guidelines in this area.

Body parts are personal, private property and should *never* be criticized on any account. The case of Laurie Les-

LIBBY REID

toil is only one in millions. Is there a woman alive who actually likes her thighs?

Breasts are also a particularly sensitive area and should be off-limits to mother's critical eye. If your daughter feels she needs a bra, do not make clever references to pancakes, floorboards, or waiting until there's something to "hold up." If your daughter doesn't want to wear a bra, do not browbeat her about feminist politics.

Similarly all discussions of body weight are totally forbidden in any context. Telling your daughter she is gaining weight is absolutely *verboten*, even in her eighth month of pregnancy. Mothers should also be careful about commenting on weight loss, as this will only make your daughter wonder, "Was I so much fatter the last time I saw Mom?"

Strictly speaking, a child's eating habits fall under the domain of allowable parental supervision, and most mothers waste a great deal of time and energy attempting to promote healthy food choices to their offspring. Unfortunately children are adept at pointing out the hypocrisy of a parent's best efforts in this area. Children know that as soon as they are asleep, Mom is tearing away the cellophane on the Oreos. True, by day Mom lives on chicken salad and melba toast, but kids know that by nightfall Mom has her soup spoon in the Häagen-Dazs.

The dinner table can be a battleground of parent-child conflict. This is because mothers do not realize that each child has a TMIQ (Table Manners Intelligence Quotient). TMIQ has nothing to do with a child's ability in math, science, or language arts. Your child may be extremely smart. Still, there's a limit to how much table manners she or he can actually learn. Most children peak at the age of seven. After that they simply cannot absorb another parental demand concerning how fast or in what manner their food is consumed. This is why you still see forty-year-old men talking with their mouth full or a grandmother playing with her food. Accept your child's TMIQ limitation and her elbows on the table. If she no longer spits food across the dining room, consider yourself among the fortunate.

Don't bother criticizing your daughter's use of the telephone. This is, perhaps, a mother's most monumental waste of time. Your daughter will never get off the phone, and she will eventually wear you down into getting her her own telephone line. This one's inevitable, so save your breath.

Do not be critical of your daughter's friends, especially her male companions. Maternal complaints concerning unsuitable boyfriends will only make those characters even more appealing in the eyes of your impressionable daughter. In addition remember that high school is only a transitory phase in the life cycle of your child. Think about the guys you dated in high school and the girls who were your closest friends back then. How many of these people are still on your Christmas list?

Punctuality is a major issue for adults, but it is not an area of great concern to children. Yes, you can get your child washed, dressed, fed, and out the door by 8:15, but you cannot ensure that she will make it to third-period Biology by the time the bell rings. Contrary to popular parental belief, tardiness is not one of the cardinal sins.

Also avoid derogatory comments about hair, nails, skin, and makeup. A comment such as "You look like you stuck your finger in a light socket" will *not* encourage your daughter to run off to the hairdresser for a new do.

Fashion trends come and go, but daughters should feel free to express themselves through clothes and shoes without Mom's advice or criticism. As any girl-child knows, making a fashion statement, however seemingly misdirected, can help you survive many of life's traumas. Phyllis Theroux has written brilliantly on this theme in the short story "Johanna's First Day at School":

> In my daughter's fourth-grade class there are fifteen girls. With the exception of Johanna, they are all fairly desperate to be exactly like every little girl there. But that is not possible for Johanna. She is, first of all, twenty pounds heavier than anyone else in the class. She is taller, biracial, adopted, and neither brilliant nor a joke teller. Circumstances have come together to make her different, and Johanna might have crept into school on the first day, looking

neither left nor right, hoping that all these strikes would not be held against her. She did no such thing.

Johanna stood on the school steps like a self-satisfied princess, wearing a long pink nylon dress—one of her mother's nightgowns—tied around the waist with a wide piece of pink satin blanket binding. She had chosen to wear over her nightgown-dress—rightly so, I thought—a white knitted cape with tasseled fringe. Then, since one always needs accessories, to complement the main idea she had found a bright-pink plastic headband with an eternally pink bow set on top of her dark brown curly hair. Johanna stood out on the front steps like a peony among tweed suits.

I watched Johanna and read on her face a look of satisfaction that was neither arrogant nor silly. The fact is that Johanna looked absolutely ravishing. I knew it. She knew it. Everybody knew it. But what nobody, perhaps not even Johanna, knew is how she acquired the advanced understanding that enabled her to convert a hazardous mine field into a tour de force.

Johanna had turned the first day of school on its ear.

If your daughter, like Johanna, feels the need to express her individuality through seemingly inappropriate apparel, do not criticize. (After all, look how well it works for Cher.) Get out your nightgowns and rejoice.

ACCEPTABLE CRITICISMS

Contrary to what moms often say ("I can't tell my daughter anything!"), there are a few topics available for criticism—as long as moms don't get carried away with themselves.

Mom may feel free to criticize her daughter's messy room or untidy habit of leaving stuff all over the house. Daughters have heard these criticisms so often that, after the age of five, they simply fail to register.

It is also permissible to voice a negative opinion about permanent tattoos and liposuction, especially if your daughter is under the age of ten.

THE ABSOLUTE DON'T

If you cannot control your urge to criticize your daughter (many women can't), you must at least follow this absolute maxim: Never, Never, Never voice an opinion about your daughter in front of another human being. This is only adding humiliation to injury.

During a gathering of your friends, do not discuss your daughter's bathing or grooming habits. Never discuss anything with your daughter's date other than the time or weather. One mother in Cleveland deeply regrets the night she asked her daughter's date, "Doesn't Sybil look lovely in her new sweater? She bought it just for tonight." Sadly (but understandably) this poor mother never heard from Sybil again.

WAIT TO BE ASKED

If your daughter wants your opinion, she'll ask for it. But remember that you are skating on thin emotional ice if she says, "I really, really want to know what you think. Be totally honest. How do I look?"

In answering this loaded question, be mindful of how you reacted to your mother's opinion and follow this general rule of thumb: Your daughter desperately wants your opinion as long as it exactly concurs with her opinion.

Tell her she looks fabulous, even if you are lying through your teeth.

If she says, "You're just saying that because you're my mother," tell her, "Even if you were a stranger on the street or someone I really hated, I'd still have to say, '*That girl looks fabulous. She must be a model. I wonder where she bought that wonderful blouse.*'"

If you can be convincing, maybe your daughter will ask for your opinion again before you are a great-grandmother.

BONUS SECTION FOR SINGLE WOMEN

If you are still single, you face the trauma of repeatedly being asked, "Why aren't you married yet?" Single women know that Mom is not satisfied until she has asked this question at least once every half hour. It is a question that is also very popular with the surrogate mothers in a single woman's life: aunts, uncles, cousins, rabbis, priests, manicurists, former best friends, and taxi drivers.

Most women do not know how to answer this question without foaming at the mouth. So, as a service to our readers, we present twenty-three responses that can be employed the next time Mom (or her counterpart) asks, *"Why aren't you married yet?"*

1. "Mel Gibson is already taken."
2. "What? And spoil my great sex life?"
3. "I look awful in white."
4. "Because I love hearing this question."
5. "Just lucky, I guess."
6. "It's my way of giving you something to live for."
7. "I'm waiting for the state to approve my new boyfriend's parole."

8. "I'm still hoping for a shot at Miss America."
9. "Do you know how hard it is to get *two* tickets to *Phantom of the Opera?*"
10. "I think marriage takes all the spontaneity out of dating."
11. "I leave dirty underwear on the floor, *Rambo* on the VCR, and the toilet seat up to get the same effect."
12. "It didn't seem worth a blood test."
13. "I already have enough laundry to wash, thank you very much."
14. "They just opened a great new singles bar on my block."
15. "I don't want you and Dad to drop dead from happiness."
16. "Well, it just goes to prove you can't really trust those sacrificial-voodoo-doll rituals, I guess."
17. "What? And lose all the money I've invested in personal ads?"
18. "We really want to, but my boyfriend's wife won't go for it."
19. "I don't want to support another person on my paycheck."
20. "Men are only good for one thing—and I can put up my own shelves, thank you very much."
21. "I'm married to my career, although we are considering a trial separation."
22. "My last proposal was in sixth grade."
23. "Why aren't you thinner, Ma?"

ALTERNATIVE SOLUTIONS IF YOU'VE ALREADY TURNED INTO YOUR MOTHER

She reminded him of his mother. He wanted to run up and hug her and protect her, and at the same time he wanted to throw a plate at the back of her neck.

—Sarah Gilbert, *Hairdo*

SEEKING NONPROFESSIONAL HELP: THE NINE-STEP PROGRAM

Many professionals—doctors, psychiatrists, psychologists, and high school guidance counselors—have argued that the fear of turning into your mother is more than a psychiatric obsession. Many people feel this condition is a bona fide disease, which they have named Mamaholism.

Mamaholism is defined as a condition whereby a woman is powerless over her mother.

For years these women refused to admit they were anything at all like their mothers. They lived in a state of total denial (which is even worse than living in the state of New Jersey).

There is no simple cure for Mamaholism, and some people feel the disease is in fact incurable because, remember, the situation began before you, the victim, were even born. From the moment of your conception, perhaps even before, your mother was planning your future and plotting ways to marry you off to a dermatologist.

However, there is a group of women who understands the problem and has learned to cope with its symptoms. They are called Mamaholics Anonymous (MA).

The first step in joining MA is to recognize your problem by standing up and saying, perhaps for the first time in your life, "My name is _____, and I am just like my mother."

The second step is to make a list of all the things Mom has ever done to you that were mean, rotten, or just plain unfair. Each Mamaholic must become willing to share these shortcomings with her mother.

Third, it is important to attend regular MA meetings and to share your complaints with other women. In this way we come to realize that we are not alone in wishing that Mom would move to another continent, even though we love her very much.

The formal rules and guidelines of Mamaholics Anonymous are outlined in *My MA Book,* which is available for purchase at all meetings. For spiritual guidance, members refer to *Gone with the Wind* because it is the only book everyone has read.

The history of MA dates back well into 1985. It began with just two women sharing coffee and complaints about their mothers. Soon other women joined, until today MA has so many members, they're too big for their britches.

The women meet often because many of them do not date very much.

Each meeting begins with a general discussion about how everybody looks. Members note if anyone has cut their bangs, is wearing new shoes, or has cramps. If there's any time left for the meeting, they begin by reading aloud "The MA Preamble":

> Mamaholics Anonymous is a fellowship of gals who share their experience, strength, hope, and cashmere sweaters with each other so that they may solve their common problems and help others to recover from Mamaholism.
>
> The sole requirement for joining MA is the desire *not* to turn out like your mother.
>
> MA is not allied with any sect, denomination, politics, organization, or institution except for Bloomingdale's and Häagen-Dazs to whom we may turn when we can't get Mom off the phone. We believe in only one affiliation: Call Waiting.
>
> Our primary purpose is to realize that (a) we don't have to be like our mothers; and (b) Mom wasn't so bad after all.

Following the reading, members review the Nine Guidelines that form the basis of MA. All members are required to memorize the guidelines because occasionally they are given a spot quiz.

THE NINE GUIDELINES OF MA

1. We remain anonymous, because if we didn't, our mothers would kill us.
2. Everyone is encouraged to stand up and speak at our meetings, although if you can't say anything nice about someone, you probably shouldn't say anything at all.
3. Meetings are free, although it wouldn't hurt if you brought along a box of Danish or a nice coffee cake.

4. If you are late getting to a meeting, we get fed up with you.
5. If you have to miss a meeting, you could at least call and tell us you're not coming.
6. No professional or paraprofessional counselors run MA therapy groups, because so many of our members are professional and paraprofessional counselors.
7. Dress is casual, but clean underwear is absolutely required at all times. Jeans are permissible, although it wouldn't kill you to put on a skirt. A little panty girdle wouldn't hurt either. And what, in heaven's name, have you done to your hair?
8. Our group is self-supporting because MasterCard turned down our application.
9. There are no dues, because no matter how much you offered to pay, it couldn't come close to repaying us for all we've done for you.

DISCUSSIONS

MA meetings consist mainly of informal discussions and formal complaining where everyone tells stories about their mother.

Each meeting focuses on a particular problem of concern to Mamaholics: Sex, Needing Mother's Approval, Sex, Repeating Our Mistakes, Sex, What Our Dreams Mean, Sex, Our Therapists, and of course problems about Sex.

USING THE SERENDIPITY PRAYER

After every meeting all members join hands and take a moment to give thanks for MA by reciting the Serendipity Prayer.

On the walls of thousands of MA meeting rooms, in any variety of languages, this invocation can be seen:

Mom, grant me the serendipity to accept the things about you that you cannot change,

The courage to remind you what you can change,

And the wisdom to keep my mouth shut about your new hair color!

For many members serendipity seemed like an impossible goal when they came into the program. But most members eventually learn that when things get really tough, they can always go shopping, which is why, after reciting the Serendipity Prayer, all members squeeze each other's hands and enthusiastically remind themselves, "Keep coming back, eventually Donna Karan will go on sale!"

SEEKING PROFESSIONAL HELP: ANALYSIS, PARALYSIS

Don't think you're free from becoming your mother simply because your mom was a June Cleaver clone who baked oatmeal cookies for your Brownie meetings. Psychiatrists will confirm that, in all probability, your mom still had no feeling for your inner emotional world, which is why today you are compelled to date only men who treat you like a sack of potatoes.

The purpose of psychoanalysis is to release you from idealizing your childhood, thus allowing you to feel genuine contempt for Mom, perhaps for the first time in your life.

To cure yourself completely, you will have to spend a decade or two in intensive therapy, at least three times a week. You will undergo a process called transference, which means you will take all your feelings for your mother and transfer them to your therapist. Soon you will feel great contempt for your therapist.

In analysis there are four basic areas on which you will have to concentrate. Simplified somewhat for the purpose of easy access, the following levels chart your course through analysis.

LEVEL A: ADMIT THAT YOU WERE MISERABLE AS A CHILD.

Forget all those happy childhood memories. Psychiatrists will tell you that you are repressing the pain. It doesn't matter how you consciously remember your childhood, in order to please your shrink, you must confess that you were totally, painfully, inconsolably unhappy as a child.

LEVEL B: REPEAT YOUR CHILDHOOD.

With the help of your therapist, you will attempt to re-create the misery of your lost infancy and youth. You will rediscover how difficult it was to deal with the loneliness of your childhood, especially because you were too little at the time to undo the cap on the vodka.

LEVEL C: DEVELOP YOUR INTELLECT, DECREASE YOUR EMOTIONS.

You will learn to intellectualize everything so that nothing can hurt you and to keep all of your emotions safely at arm's length. (Or, wait a minute, is it the other way around?)

LEVEL D: EXCEL BRILLIANTLY IN EVERYTHING AND ADMIRE YOURSELF GREATLY FOR YOUR ACHIEVEMENTS.

You are cured! To quote the last line from *Jane Fonda's Workout Record,* "Don't you feel better? See you next time!"

━━━━━

In all probability you will have no trouble with any of these levels. Perhaps it should be noted, however, that these are only the levels you transcend during your first fifteen minutes in analysis. The remaining ten years and thirty-five minutes are a bit more complicated, especially when you get to the part where you have to talk about your feelings toward your shrink and your running tab.

The best part about analysis, however, is that you will be able to discover how truly neurotic you are. This information can change your life or, at the very least, your career. As has been proven, if you are really, really deranged and were genuinely traumatized in childhood, after analysis you are forty-seven times more likely to become a psychologist yourself.

QUESTIONS AND ANSWERS: A NOTED PSYCHIATRIST TALKS ABOUT MOTHERS AND DAUGHTERS

In this chapter Dr. Mildred Gittlestein shares with us many of the questions that her patients ask every day, day after day, during the course of their therapy. "I thought that if we wrote down the questions and the answers, my patients would stop pestering me already," says Dr. Gittlestein.

Question: With my mother I never seem to do anything right. Why does she expect so much from me?

Answer: It is not unusual for mothers to set superhuman standards for their daughters. Mom wants you to be all the things she wasn't. If you fail, she resents you. If you succeed, she resents you even more.

————

Q: I have trouble talking to my mother. I try to be open and honest with her, but she doesn't listen to me. Instead of having a meaningful dialogue, we always wind up yelling at each other. What can we do?

A: I am so sick and tired of all this whining about communication and meaningful dialogues. Where is it written that mothers and daughters have to share every little detail of their lives? Mothers and daughters need to understand that there are certain topics they should never discuss with each other. Why do you think best friends and sisters were invented?

For instance, off the top of my head, here is a list of some of the things you should never tell your mother:

- You ever had sex.
- You aren't wearing clean underwear.
- You aren't wearing *any* underwear.
- You don't believe in marriage.
- You lied about the dog breaking her Waterford vase in 1968.
- Your new boyfriend is married.
- You used to wish she were more like your aunt Gladys.
- You never really liked her oatmeal cookies.
- She was right about a lot of stuff.

THE MOTHER/DAUGHTER RELATIONSHIP
CROSSING THE SEA of CONFLICT

UNSOLICITED ADVICE
PEER GROUP PRESSURE
INAPPROPRIATE BOYFRIENDS
SURPRISE INSULTS
THE GOOD PARTS
BAD MOODS
SHARED FEARS

LIBBY REID

Take my advice, stick to discussions about hemlines, the movies, the next-door neighbors, and your father's stupid relatives. Believe me, life will be a lot easier.

Q: All my friends love my mother and I love most of my best friends' mothers. Why don't I feel as good about my own mom? Why do other people's moms seem so terrific?

A: Think of it as an optical illusion. What you see in other people's moms is not always what you get, because you are basing your judgment on the "when company is around" behavioral factor. Seeing other moms without visitors in the house is like seeing them without makeup. You never really know what to expect.

███████

Q: My best friend says my problem is that I'm always putting myself down. Of course that's easy for her to say, because she has, like, a perfect body and really great hair. I mean, I could diet forever and never look like her on her worst day. And forget my hair. Like, two hundred bucks in perms and dye jobs and I still look like Little Orphan Annie. What am I supposed to do?

A: Have you thought about getting a different best friend?

Only kidding. Seriously, I would say that you do seem to have a problem with self-esteem, which I am certain comes from your childhood experiences, because clearly you are used to putting yourself down.

No one has to learn how to put herself down, especially when Mom is around. Sometimes it seems as though Mom's full-time job is looking for your faults and shortcomings and, once she finds them, reminding you of those deficiencies five or six times a day.

You know, you can grow up and leave home, but somehow you take all those criticisms with you. When Mom's not around, you assume her job and put yourself down—at least until the time when you have kids and can concentrate on their shortcomings.

███████

Q: Why couldn't my mom be more like Donna Reed?

A: Darling, in real life Donna Reed wasn't like Donna Reed.

Unfortunately we are the generation raised on popular TV moms like Donna Reed, Harriet Nelson, Jane Wyman, and Florence Brady.

Compared with these holy shrines of motherhood, our own mothers seemed petty, negligent, uninspiring, and ill groomed. The perfectly coiffed TV mom with her starched apron and string of pearls was perpetually baking cookies, ever on call to her children. Understanding, sympathetic, devoted, loving, and patient, TV moms never lectured, never got really angry, never fell victim to PMS. At best they sent a naughty child to his bedroom, only to sneak in milk and cookies before the next commercial interruption.

Recently I participated in a study of another famous TV mom: Lucille Ball. The following citation is from the minutes of a weekend conference on childrearing held at the Children of the Channels (COC) Research Center in Santa Cruz, California:

> Because Lucille Ball virtually gave birth to Little Ricky on national television, many young mothers over-identified with the red-haired comedienne. Fifties moms routinely played Lucy with their kids by pretending to work in a chocolate factory or to audition for a spot in the chorus line. Often these children were encouraged to cry with their mouths open and to make fun of Daddy's diction.

The COC Research Center also noted that the popularity of the *I Love Lucy* Childrearing Method during the late 1950s and early 1960s explains why today so many forty-year-old men enjoy wearing red lipstick and dressing up like Carmen Miranda.

But enough of this digression. To return to your original question, I believe that the past was the past, and you should realize that in the 1980s Donna Reed didn't last two seasons as Miss Ellie on *Dallas*.

For all you know, Donna Reed might have turned into the most nagging mom in TV syndication. Don't live in the past. Reruns are reruns.

Twenty years from now do you want your daughter asking, "Why couldn't my mom be more like Mel Harris?"

■■■■■

Q: I've always suffered from low self-esteem. My mom always told me that looks aren't everything and that I'd never be a brain surgeon. My daughter told me I needed to grow as a person. So for the past few years I've been very busy.

I mean, I've done it all: est, assertiveness training, Silva Mind Control, analysis, astrology, PTA, Al-Anon, P.E.T., TM, oat bran, yoga, crystals, Oprah, reincarnation, and mammograms. I've kept journals and written down every problem and emotion. I am fully self-actualized. I'm my own best friend, a Total Woman, and I've talked to the animals. I've worked through my childhood, the Cinderella syndrome, the Peter Pan complex, the Peter Principle, and my numerous former lives. I've communicated with every member of my family, as well as several families down the block. I've raised my consciousness and my self-esteem. I've rolfed and rolled. I've lived in a geodesic dome and done time in an isolation tank. I've left my body and traveled on an astral plane. I even bought a co-op when the market was down.

Now I've decided that it's time to stop growing as a person. In fact I've grown all I care to.

The problem is my family hasn't gotten any less critical. My mom says I still act like a child and my daughter
thinks I should get my thighs suctioned. Is there anything I
can do to please them?

A: No.

SEEKING SELF-HELP: STOP MOTHERING YOURSELF

Inside your head there are many little voices. These voices tell you what to do, what to say, and when to water your plants. These different voices have conversations with each other. You ask yourself an innocent question and then answer it, sort of like movie dialogue, with you playing all of the roles. "When was the last time I had Chinese?" you might ask yourself. "Lunch," you reply.

We all have conversations with ourselves. They begin almost from the moment we wake up in the morning. For example the alarm rings at 6:30 A.M. and you ask yourself, "Why do I have to get up?" You hit the snooze button and fall asleep before you can answer. Five minutes later the buzzer rings again and you answer your own question: "I have to get up so that I can wake my husband, wake my children, take a shower, make breakfast, put on a suit from my 'fat' wardrobe that probably won't fit anyway since I seem to be retaining water like crazy, dress the kids, yell and scream at everyone, drive the kids to school, and rush downtown to fight with my boss. I think we're out of milk. Did I remind Jim he has a dentist appointment this morning? Did Melissa finish her homework last night? Will they let Nancy die of cancer on *Thirtysomething*? What time is it anyway?" By now you discover you are a half hour behind schedule. If you could learn to cut your inner conversations to a minimum, you might have time to wash your hair in the morning.

Try this tomorrow morning: As soon as the alarm goes off, say to yourself, "My life is a mess," and get out of bed.

Many people do not admit that they have these inner conversations. That's why these inner conversations are sometimes called thinking. The term "thinking" is unknown to some (your garage mechanic, for instance), but to almost anyone the word is more palatable than the idea of inner conversations. In our society it's undeniably true that "I was just thinking out loud" carries more validity than "I was talking to myself."

Actually when we carry on these conversations, we are not really talking to ourselves. In point of fact we are talking to our mothers.

While there are many different voices in your head — the voice of reason, the voice of sanity, and the voice of practicality — by far the loudest (and most critical) is the voice of your mother.

Yes, even when she's not in the room or on the phone, a convenient travel-sized mom rides along in the crevices of your mind. Underneath your husband's shirt size and the beginnings of that PTA speech you have to deliver on Tuesday is a Miniature Mom telling you what to do and how to do it. If you could pull back your gray matter, the way you'd peel a ripe fig, you'd discover Miniature Mom perched on your frontal lobe. She's firmly entrenched in your brain, fulfilling her maternal obligation to undermine your self-esteem, even though she's only doing it for your own good.

The really weird part is that Miniature Mom is not alone. Keeping her company inside your brain is The Little Girl You Once Were. No matter how old we get, that little girl still lives within us. Yes, she's still there—pouting, whining, and trying not to die of embarrassment. She's the reason why you still lust after James Dean, enjoy playing dress-up, get totally into playing Clue with your kids, and occasionally feel the urge to climb the jungle gym or belly flop down the sliding pond. You refrain from some of these more physical activities of course, because as soon as the idea crosses your brain, Miniature Mom pipes in, "What? At your age? Are you nuts?"

It should come as no shock that these inner conversations bear a striking resemblance to the actual conversations you have with your real-life mother. It's a well-documented fact that Miniature Mom and The Little Girl You Once Were are constantly bickering with each other, just like in your childhood.

To prove the point, let's review a typical conversation between Miniature Mom (MM) and The Little Girl You Once Were (TLGYOW) that probably took place within your brain sometime during the past two weeks.

TLGYOW: I want to buy this dress.
MM: Purple is not your color, dear.
TLGYOW: It's just the lights in this dressing room.
MM: You don't have any shoes to wear with purple.
TLGYOW: I'll buy new shoes.

MM: You can't afford both the dress and the shoes. Not
　　 with the salary you make at that stupid job.

TLGYOW: I'll charge it.

MM: Sure, get deeper in debt, Miss Never-Save-a-Dime.

TLGYOW: But if Tom asks me out, I may need a dressy
　　 dress.

MM: Don't count your chickens before they're hatched.

TLGYOW: Well, it's possible he'll ask me out, and even if he
　　 doesn't, I'll feel much better wearing something
　　 new.

MM: You always had your head in the clouds.

TLGYOW: (Sigh) Maybe you're right. Perhaps I shouldn't
　　 spend all this money.

MM: Better you should buy yourself a warm winter coat.

TLGYOW: Anyway it doesn't fit all that well.

MM: It pulls along the backside.

TLGYOW: Tomorrow I'll go on a diet and lose fifteen
　　 pounds.

MM: Tomorrow I'll be crowned queen of England.

TLGYOW: The material is really beautiful, though.

MM: It probably has to be dry-cleaned.

TLGYOW: I don't *really* need it.

MM: My feet hurt. Can't we go get coffee someplace?

　　 In this situation you must decide between pleasing that
Little Girl You Once Were and pleasing your Miniature
Mom. You can choose one of the following:

a. Please yourself and buy the dress.
b. Please your Miniature Mom and don't buy the dress.
　　 Of course there is always the third option: Buy the
dress, the new shoes, and a warm winter coat. Borrow
the money from your mother. You'll feel guilty (but well
dressed). She'll feel extravagant and have you indebted

to her (her favorite combination of emotions). Everyone wins.

HOW TO GET RID OF MINIATURE MOM

These inner conversations with Miniature Mom rule our lives and our wardrobes. Our closets are filled with warm winter coats that we bought only to get Miniature Mom off our back. We are so used to validating our own opinions to Mom that these arguments continue even after we moved five hundred miles away from home.

Is there a cure?

Experts tell us that we can take control of our inner conversations. Dr. Mildred Gittlestein, in her landmark paper "If You Can't Say Anything Nice to Yourself, Don't Say Anything at All," offers this simple solution: "Tell your Miniature Mom to shut up!"

Of course the problem is that this is as hard to do in your head as it is in real life. Many of us are afraid to follow this simple advice, remembering all the time we spent in our rooms for being disrespectful. So if you can't make Miniature Mom shut up, do yourself a favor and send her on a vacation. Offer her a trip to Miami Beach. (Use your Frequent Flyer miles if money is tight.) Or if MM hates the sun, ship her off to Aunt Ida's in Peoria. Be kind but be firm.

Tell her you need some time to yourself, even though this ploy rarely works with mothers. Once her children are of college age or beyond, no mother can grasp the concept of spending time alone. It seemed important when she had four toddlers constantly underfoot, but that changed once her children grew up into interesting adults who could carry their end of a conversation.

Now Mom can't get enough of you. She's always

complaining that you're rushing off just to avoid being with her. "What's the matter?" she'll say. "You'd rather go for an emergency root canal than have tea with your old mother?" (Give her credit, Mom's accusations are often right on target.)

Anyway the point is that MM has to go. If all else fails, you can always tell her you need space to do some spring cleaning. "I've got to vacuum behind those gray cells. You'll just be in the way."

Once MM has departed, you'll be amazed at the changes in your life. You'll be able to eat an entire box of Milk Duds without worrying about cavities. You may not change your sheets for a whole month. You won't even notice those split ends.

But be forewarned. MMs have the habit of returning to the scene of the crime, usually when you least expect them.

You'll be happily reading that trashy novel at 2:30 in the morning when a little voice rings out, "You're ruining your eyes with that light."

You sigh. "Welcome home, Ma," you say before closing the book and turning out the light.

SEEKING LEGAL HELP: CONTRACTUAL AGREEMENTS

From the moment of your conception you entered into a legally binding contractual arrangement with your mother. Naturally this was a nonverbal agreement, since you (as a fetus) were too small at the time to negotiate the finer points or read the small print of this lifelong contract. Under the obligations of your Prenatal Agreement, you and your mother contracted to do the following:

> The party of the first part, *Mother,* agrees to go through labor and give birth to you. She will provide food, love, comfort, clothing, and, occasionally, trips to Disneyland and McDonald's.
>
> The party of the second part, *Daughter,* will endeavor to be the cutest baby ever born. She will worship her mother, listen to her every word, and provide said mother with all the respect and admira-

tion she never received from her mother. In return
for being born, daughter also contracts to care for
mother when she is really old. Daughter understands
that this contract shall be legal and binding until the
day she draws her last breath on earth.

At the time this seems like a fair deal for both parties,
but most lawyers will tell you that, at the signing of any
contract, most parties think the agreement is fair. Take
Donald Trump, for example. It is only after the ink dries
that one of the parties involved first becomes suspicious.
Take Ivana Trump, for example.

Of course you did not understand that you were en-
tering into a lifelong obligation by allowing yourself to be
born. If you had, you might never have agreed to vacate
the womb. Or at the very least you would have insisted on
negotiating certain legal privileges, such as the right to wear
white lipstick and torn jeans without suffering a lot of maternal grief.

As your legal guardian your mother was entitled to
enter you into this binding agreement without your prior
consent. And all goes well under the terms of this agreement for approximately six months. Then the daughter
usually starts breaking the rules by developing a personality
that is in conflict with Mom's. "I never agreed to put up
with colic!" many mothers complain to their lawyers.

ADDENDA

Although it was never formally notarized, or even verbal-
ized, your contract with Mom continued to expand and
adjust as you grew. Certain addenda were added to your
contract. These addenda vary within different families, but
some typical clauses include the following:

- Mother consents to read the same Dr. Seuss story 437 times. Daughter agrees to be potty trained.
- Mother is permitted to bring a rival sibling into the household, and in exchange daughter gets a later bed-time.
- Mother provides ballet and piano lessons; daughter agrees to practice.
- Mother grants the privilege of sleep-overs and daughter molds an "I Love My Mommy" clay ashtray in arts and crafts.

Children soon realize the limitations of their legal rights as more and more things are fostered upon them without their approval, written or otherwise. These include school, religion, shoes with proper support, haircuts, baby-sitters, rainwear, bedtime, toothbrushes, checkups, boring family stuff, baths, table manners, and cough medicine. Mothers claim that all of these items fall within the general This-Is-Good-for-You codicil, an invariable part of every mother-daughter contractual agreement.

LAWSUITS

Once the child learns to speak, most mothers and daughters realize that the terms of their agreement must be re-negotiated. Daughters are granted the privilege of saying two mean things a year to mom without being punished, with the stipulation that this privilege can be revoked if the daughter uses up her lifetime quota before graduating kindergarten. Mothers, as we all know, feel no legal constriction in the inconsiderate-remarks department under the "What did I say wrong this time?" clause in their contract. This point of law was recently tested in the courts when a real estate agent named Kimberly DeMato sued her mother in small-claims court in the state of North Dakota. The following transcript is taken directly from Ms. De-Mato's court testimony:

"Your Honor, on May 23rd, 1986, at approximately 1:30 P.M., I received, by mail, my real estate license. I was really excited about it. I mean, you know, this was a real accomplishment for me. It took me almost six months to study for the exam.

"I can't tell you how great it felt just to hold that license in my hot little hands. Now, my mother's standing right there next to me when the mailman arrived, so I said to her, 'Look, Mom, isn't this just too fabulous for words?'

"My mother glances at the license, kind of shrugs, and in that voice of hers says, 'Oh, Kimberly, if only your sister, Annie, was a real estate agent, what a fortune *she* could earn!' "

Naturally Kimberly's mom pleaded maternal ignorance in court. In her deposition brief she stated, "I don't know what was so terrible about what I said. My Kimberly, gosh, that child is just so sensitive. Everything I say to her becomes a federal case."

The judge in the lawsuit declared that he was "not empowered to handle federal cases," and kicked the suit out of his court. Kimberly's case is now pending in the Supreme Court.

WRITING A NEW CONTRACT

Much of the confusion between mothers and daughters stems from the fact that their contractual agreement is never formally spelled out. They go through life bound to a little-understood but completely binding invisible document. Therefore many lawyers advise quarreling mothers and daughters to draw up a new contract. Ivy Peterson, a lawyer practicing maternal law in Newport Beach, California, recommends that mothers and daughters sit down and hammer out an agreement that clearly defines their legal rights and obligations toward each other. "Get it in writing," advises Ivy. "Some families balk at the idea of a written contract, but I say to them, Listen, people draw up prenuptial agreements before getting married, and let's face it, no marriage ever lasts as long as your relationship with your mother."

Ivy offers her clients several tips for successfully negotiating a contract. First, she says, pick a good time to talk, not when either party is on the phone or dressing to go out. Second, be specific about your needs and remember that "Your life is going down the toilet!" does not constitute constructive criticism. Third, listen to each other. "It's this third one that gets most moms," sighs Ivy, "but I keep it on the list anyway."

The idea of drawing up a contract may seem intimidating to some mothers and daughters until they consider the people they know who are practicing lawyers.

It is actually a very simple procedure as long as you have a blank contract to follow, which is exactly what we provide in the next few pages. This sample contract includes the general format of a typical mother-daughter contract plus several tips on how to negotiate specific points.

SAMPLE

MOTHER-DAUGHTER CONTRACT

This agreement, dated _____, between (mother) _____ and (daughter) _____ shall be legal and binding, even when we're really mad at each.

Whereas, the parties jointly desire to build a better relationship; and

Whereas, each party has to live in the same house (town, city, planet, etc.); and

Whereas, each party agrees to follow the dictates of this Agreement even if one of the parties does eventually marry someone who is not in the medical or legal profession;

Now, Therefore, both Parties agree as follows:

I.
CLEANLINESS.

There are two major points to negotiate in this clause: (a) the amount of cleaning, which has a variable from once a month to once every half hour; and (b) the degree of cleaning, from light dusting to down-on-all-fours scrubbing. Parties shall discuss and put into writing addenda covering dishes, general clutter, bathroom fixtures, kitchen appliances, making beds, changing sheets, taking out the garbage, laundry, and domestic help.

2.
MUSIC.

Set limitations on specific stereo decibel readings (from 1 to 10); types of music; and when, and if, musical instruments shall be practiced. Parties may also wish to cover dial settings on car radios in this clause.

3.
TV VIEWING.

This clause covers types of programming, from police dramas about cocaine busts to educational shows, acceptable amounts of TV viewing, an allowance for cable programming, tape rental, and Nintendo games. It should be noted that this clause is often the most difficult to negotiate because mothers and daughters have gigantic differences of opinion in this particular area. But, according to Ms. Peterson, it is extremely important to iron out this clause. "When clients can't come to terms on this clause, I always cite the case of the Minneapolis woman who was charged with bludgeoning to death her seventy-eight-year-old mother because Mom insisted on watching *Who's the Boss?* when *Look Who's Talking* was showing on HBO."

4.
SEX.

Both parties agree to never discuss.

5.
FAIRNESS.

Both parties, but especially mother, agree to work very hard to achieve a satisfactory level of fairness in the home. This means that mom will not allow siblings to get away with murder, and daughter will refrain from comparing mom to every other mother on the block.

6.
VISITATION RIGHTS.

Both parties should decide what kinds of visits from acquaintances will be permitted, from prayer breakfasts to midnight biker-gang gatherings. Discuss allowable activities, from playing mah-jongg to making out in the basement.

7.
CHILDREN.

Daughters agree to provide grandchildren. This point is nonnegotiable, although some daughters have managed to add conditional clauses regarding free baby-sitting.

8.
MONEY.

Allowances and credit lines for major Gold cards should be established. Also, because of concessions granted in Clause 7, some daughters have insisted that this clause also include loans for down payments on future mortgages.

9.
MODESTY.

This clause is used by most daughters to insist that mom stop walking around the house naked.

Some mothers use this clause to define allowable bikini measurements.

10.
SCHEDULES.

Mother agrees to be responsible for getting daughter out of bed in the morning, although she is not allowed to use violence in the process. Permission to sleep till noon on weekends and school holidays is granted by some mothers (but not all).

11.
TEMPERAMENT.

Decibel readings for yelling and screaming should be established (from mildly annoyed to madder-than-hell). It is also advisable to establish a statute of limitations on holding a grudge (limited to ten years in most states, although recent legislation in California permits this statute to continue "till hell freezes over").

12.
FOOD.

Preparation is a mother's domain and consumption is a daughter's, although this tends to shift with the passage of time. Some mothers have used this clause to require daughters to eat green vegetables, but have found it a difficult rule to enforce. Burping, use of toothpicks, and dental floss at the table should be negotiated between parties.

13.
MAJOR CONVENIENCES.

Parties should agree on the frequency and use of air conditioners, window openings, and furnace settings. The use of mom's car and daughter's diffuser can be included in this clause.

14.
HOUSEHOLD PETS.

Define responsibilities and who gets final say in choice of name.

15.
DESIGNER CLOTHES.

If mother and daughter can wear the same size, they should negotiate the fine art of sharing clothes. Points to cover include the use of perfume, repairing damages, permissibility of jewelry, storing, cleaning, and returning to the rightful owner.

16.
DISPUTES.

In the event of a dispute, both parties agree to (a) cool off; (b) look for an alternative solution; (c) take the dispute to nonbinding arbitration to be conducted by a mutually-agreed-upon individual; and (d) go shopping together.

17.
AMENDMENTS.

All additions to this contract shall be made in writing with approval of both Parties and Daddy.

In witness Whereof, the undersigned set down their names on the day and year set forth above.

_____   _____
Mother   Daughter

THE LAST WORD

All women become like their mothers.
That is their tragedy. No man does.
That's his.

—Oscar Wilde
The Importance of Being Earnest

In her book *It's Always Something* the late, great Gilda Radner tells this prophetic story, a remembrance of her childhood days with Dibby, her nanny.

> When I was little, Dibby's cousin had a dog, just a mutt, and the dog was pregnant. I don't know how long dogs are pregnant, but she was due to have her puppies in about a week. She was out in the yard one day and got in the way of the lawn mower, and her two hind legs got cut off. They rushed her to the vet and he said, "I can sew her up, or you can put her to sleep if you want, but the puppies are okay. She'll be able to deliver the puppies."
>
> Dibby's cousin said, "Keep her alive."
>
> So the vet sewed up her backside and over the next week the dog learned to walk . . . by taking two steps in the front and flipping up her backside, and then taking two steps and flipping up her backside again. She gave birth to six little puppies, all in perfect health. She nursed them and then weaned them. And when they learned to walk, they all walked like her.

I think, in a way, we are all like Dibby's cousin's puppies: We pick up what is taught to us. At first we think it's perfectly normal and that whatever Mom does is just fine. It's only when we become aware of other people's moms

145

that we start to compare and contrast. Somehow our moms never quite match up to the moms down the block. This is especially true when we get into high school.

The truth is that every mother is also a daughter, and we can fight heredity all we want but somehow, sooner or later, it creeps up on us. We are destined to turn into our mothers.

And like Dibby's cousin's mutt, all mothers are lame in their own special way. As my mom would say, just wait until you're a mother, then you'll see what it's like.

Yes. And I should end this book by saying, "My name is Linda and I am just like my mother."